Murder & Crime
CHESHIRE

Murder & Crime

CHESHIRE

RAYMOND VICKERS

The
History
Press

The stocks, or pillory, at Nantwich. This is a modern replica on Pillory Street, where the originals once stood. Minor criminals would be sentenced to be held in this device so that people could throw rotten food, or worse, at them.

First published 2010

The History Press
The Mill, Brimscombe Port
Stroud, Gloucestershire, GL5 2QG
www.thehistorypress.co.uk

British Library Cataloguing in Publication Data.
A catalogue record for this book is available from the British Library.

ISBN 978 0 7524 4986 9

Typesetting and origination by The History Press
Printed in Great Britain
Manufacturing managed by Jellyfish Print Solutions Ltd

CONTENTS

ACKNOWLEDGEMENTS

This book was only made possible by the efforts of many people, whom I thank here. The biggest thank you goes to Matilda Richards of The History Press, for commissioning this book. Her generosity and patience are greatly appreciated.

The staff at the following libraries were extremely helpful:

Chester City Library
Crewe Library
Huddersfield Library (Local Studies)
Manchester Central Reference Library
Nantwich Library
Nantwich Museum

Prints and pictures were kindly supplied by:
Christine Goodier, Lancashire County Council Museums Service (picture of Old Ned Barlow); Shirley Schofield, Castleford Community Archives (Commanet) for picture of 38th Foot Captain; Anne Turner, Tameside Local Studies and Archives Centre, for prints illustrating the Ashton and Gorse Hall chapters; Michael Day, of Days Past (Sunnyfield) for supplying the postcards used to illustrate Chapter One (Lancaster Castle) and Chapter Sixteen (Glossop).

Needless to say, I alone am responsible for any mistakes, omissions, errors or misunderstandings in this book.

Chapter One

⇒◈⇐

The Warrington Gang, 1806

The borough of Warrington was part of the administrative county of Cheshire for a couple of decades from 1974, when local government was reorganised. The reorganisation of counties has meant it is possible for some people to live in three different counties without ever changing their address! Warrington was definitely not in Cheshire when the following cases happened, but we stretch the definition of Cheshire here because they are unusual cases, which throw light on early nineteenth-century attitudes.

They happened in the year 1806 and were tried at the assizes held in Lancaster Castle. In March, the county executioner was sentenced to death. The hangman who was sentenced to be hung was Edward Barlow, 69, for some twenty years the county's 'Jack Ketch' – a nickname for the official executioner. The original 'Jack Ketch' had been, in every sense, the headman at the Tower of London, famed for his incompetence and cruelty. One of his successors lost his head for theft.

Mr Barlow, otherwise known as 'Welsh Ned' or 'Old Ned' had dispatched dozens of people in his career, which had started in 1782. It came to an end when he was 'capitally convicted' for stealing a gelding belonging to Mr Wright of North Meols. Quite why he had taken up theft is unknown. Perhaps he thought that there was nobody in the county who could hang the county hangman.

At the opening of the later session of the Lancaster Assizes at Lancaster Castle in August, James Yates, aged 22, was tried for the rape and robbery of one Mary Hoyle. The reporter from *The Times* was rather ungallant in his description of Mary Hoyle – she was 58 'but looked twenty years older than she really was', and 'never was a person less calculated to excite passion'. A mother of twelve, her rape had been a brutal one. Yates, a married father of one, seemed unconcerned about the matter. He said he had no memory of the offence as he was drunk at the time.

It was a busy session. Defendants were also tried for robbery, forgery and 'wounding and ravishing' a woman. On the Tuesday, James Backhouse was tried for the murder of Thomas Brockbank of Cartmel. Found guilty of manslaughter, he was punished with a

fine of one shilling and six months imprisonment. One burglar was sentenced to seven years transportation. Thirteen-year-old Joseph Sumter was convicted of the manslaughter of 9-year-old James Gibson – in a fight. He was fined one shilling and sentenced to six months imprisonment.

On Friday, 22 August 1806, the presiding judge, Baron Graham, warned the Grand Jury and the public that he was going to try some people for unspeakable crimes. In one prominent crime, which would probably be tried in the session, some abhorrent details would be revealed. He lamented that such a subject should come before the public and that the unsuspecting minds of youth should be liable to be tainted by hearing such horrid facts. The Grand Jury comprised some very respectable ears, being made up of Lord Stanley and various knights and esquires. During the trials of the five, he ordered that no notes were taken by the press, and that no young persons were to be present at the proceedings. The accused became known as the Warrington Gang. The judge also ordered that no details of the trial were to be published. So, this account of a most unusual case is derived from page 439 of the Annual Register for 1806, which gave some details of the people involved, though no details were printed about their crimes.

According to the Annual Register, death sentences were given to Isaac Hitchin, aged 62, for assault with an attempt to commit an unnatural crime on John Knight, one of the richest men in Warrington. Knight was worth at least £60,000 – a considerable sum in those times. James Stockton, Thomas Fox and Joseph Holland were condemned for attempting similar assaults on a Mr Thomas Taylor. John Powell was convicted of an unnatural crime with John Wright.

The court heard how the men met on Monday and Friday evenings at the home of Isaac Hitchin. At these meetings Hitchin, Stockton, Fox and Holland all called each other 'brother'. All five men were found guilty and sentenced to death.

Another eight men were condemned to die with them. These were John Barker – for stealing six pieces of calico; Luke Lockard and John Barlow for forgery; James Sidebottom, for stealing a waistcoat (the jury had recommended mercy); Ralph Bolton, for burglary; two more forgers, Charles Johnson and Robert Thomas; and the aforementioned James Yates, for wounding and ravishing Mary Hoyle of Spotland.

The men were to be executed at the new gallows just outside Lancaster Castle. Gallows were designed to be erected in public places, as it was thought that the public should see the awful ends of criminal careers, and be scared into an honest life. At Lancaster, executions attracted crowds of up to 6,000 people, though 5,000 was the usual number.

On the day of execution, James Stockton was the first to die. He was reported as being very badly affected by his fate, his limbs hardly able to carry him to the gallows.

Lancaster Castle, c. 1904. The castle could attract up to 6,000 spectators for a public hanging.

John Powell was also 'much affected' but not as badly as Stockton. Joseph Holland – described as a man of gentlemanly appearance and of advanced years – was also in a state of great agitation, 'the contrition on his countenance truly indicated the penitence of his mind. He implored the pardon of almighty God'. Peter Higgins and Luke Lockard, the forgers, looked 'greatly dejected' as they trudged to the gallows. Counterfeiting currency was a very common crime at the time, and forgers were severely punished when caught.

James Yates, the ravisher, died on 13 September on the 'new drop' erected at the back of Lancaster Castle. A young man, Yates ran up the scaffold steps, and 'seemed little affected'. He was possibly putting on a show for the crowd.

Isaac Hitchin and Thomas Fox of the Warrington Gang were 'respited'. The executions were probably carried out by Edward Barlow. His supposition that no one could hang the hangman was correct. His capital sentence for horse theft was 'respited' to ten years imprisonment, provided he carried out the county's hangings and floggings. He died in his cell a few years later, on 9 December 1812.

Chapter Two

⊰◆⊱

My Delight on a Shiny Night, 1828

Today, Altrincham is in Greater Manchester, a prosperous suburb on the Manchester tramline. However, in the nineteenth century Altringham was a small market town. Note the two spellings – the name is still pronounced as Altringham locally, but the alternative spelling of Altrincham was settled by the railway companies in the 1840s, when the town's station was given that spelling.

Near the town is the great hall of Dunham Massey and its large estate. The property was owned by George Grey, whose family held the titles of Earl of Stamford and Warrington. Like all the great lords, the Lords Stamford were troubled by poachers and so kept a small army of gamekeepers. In nineteenth-century England there were often more gamekeepers than policemen – and the gamekeepers were armed. Battles between poachers and keepers were frequent. For example, the *Stockport Advertiser* of 2 January 1829 bemoaned the recent spate of incidents. The paper mentioned other cases in the previous few days. On the Cholmondeley (pronounced Chumlee) estate, some poachers had besieged the keepers in the hunting lodge. The poachers taunted the keepers, inviting them to come outside and fight. The keepers had wise heads on their shoulders, and wanted to keep them there, so they declined the challenge. The other incident is our present tale.

Our story starts in December 1828, at the home of William Perkins, a hardworking farm labourer. He lived in Dog Lane, near Altrincham, in accommodation he shared with his father and a lodger, 23-year-old Joseph Fenna. Fenna was also Perkins' brother-in-law.

A few days before Christmas 1828, a gang of poachers began firing at game in nearby Tatton Park shortly after 10 p.m. Plans were made by other gang members to invade Dunham Massey. These men went to pick up reinforcements.

Joseph Fenna, the lodger, was one such reinforcement. He was already up and about (having been called up by a friend, William Hewitt) when a party of ten poachers arrived at the house. One of the group, Thomas Bamford, proposed to go shooting pheasants at Burkenheath cover. Among the ten were six guns. They all set out

The River Weaver at Nantwich. The stone bridge dates from 1803. On the right, the road leads into the town centre. On the left is the road to Wales and Chester-Welsh Row. Until the 1970s the river bank here was lined with old buildings, including a mill dating from the 1790s.

about midnight for the Dunham estate, via Warburton's Bank, but on the way they unexpectedly met a group of gamekeepers at New Bridge Hollow.

Shouting 'They are gamekeepers!', William Hewitt and the others jumped over some railings and ran, followed by the keepers.

Thomas Hulbert, one of the poaching party, said to the pursuing men, 'Stand your ground or I'll shoot you.'

Thomas Bamford also said to the keepers who were following, 'D**n you, are you measured for your coffins? Will you not turn back? I'll shoot you if you do not.'

The group of poachers ran over two meadows, pursued by the keepers, and then some of the party repeated, 'Are you not turning back?' Three of the party struck guns, but none went off. The poachers ran across another field, with the indefatigable keepers following.

Bamford again said, 'Are you not for turning back yet?'

'No, we are not turning back,' was the reply.

'Then I'll shoot you,' said Bamford, and fired his gun. Joseph Fenna and Joseph Massey also fired at the keepers, but missed. The poachers turned and ran away again.

John Henshall said to Bamford, 'Put a bullet in.'

The pursuit continued to Bollenbridge, where they came to a nursery; Bamford threw one of two guns that he had (one belonging to Royle) into a plantation along

The gates at the entrance to Tatton Park, which adjoined Dunham Massey. The poaching gang were hunting on both estates that fateful night.

with the incriminating evidence – the pheasant. They then returned to Bank Hall. Bamford said, 'We may as well turn again, they will follow us home.'

Hulbert, Bamford and Massey turned back about two woods [*sic*] away. Bamford again said to the keepers, 'Are you not for turning back?' Bamford, Hussey and Hulbert then fired their guns, which were levelled at the keepers, who were about 21 yards off. Perkin was about two roods from Bamford and the others. At the later trial, Perkins claimed that they had bullets to shoot the keepers' dogs rather than the keepers. He also said that 'when we ran away we wanted to go home. We should have gone to Warburton's Bank, if we had not seen the keepers; but when we had seen them, we should have gone home if they had not followed us. The keepers said "Joseph [Fenna, the prisoner] thou mayst as well stop, we know thee." However, some of the poachers taunted the keepers, shouting, 'You may as well turn back.'

At that time, many farmers and landowners kept a kennel of fierce guard dogs to deter poachers and thieves. However, Lord Stamford's keepers had sporting dogs, but no fierce man-chasing dogs.

Fenna and his party ran away so as not to be recognised, so they did not head for home immediately, but went by a roundabout route through the countryside to shake off the keepers.

For the keepers' side of the story, Mr Daniel Shaw, gamekeeper, said that on 22 December he had assembled a large party of men, fifteen in number, for the protection of the game. He heard guns fired at about half past ten that night. That must have been the group who raided the Tatton estate. He went to Warburton's Bank and asked his men to meet him there. They all met up at around half past eleven. Mr Shaw left his party there, and went off to the toll bar at Newbridge, about 200 yards away. Then he returned to his party, and they concealed themselves until about 2 a.m. The guns had then ceased and he desired the men to follow him one by one; they did so up to Newbridge, where they saw a body of men, about ten or twenty in number. It was then rather overcast. Thomas Yarwood, one of the keepers' group, said, 'They are going.' He told the court:

> We saw them leave the road and go over into a field. We pursued them, and when we came within 80 or 100 yards, they all turned and ran away, and we pursued them. I judged the country they came from and ran toward a bridge, but the waters being out, I found I had overshot my way and missed my party. I had a double barrelled gun with me. There was another gun in our party, and we had a dog – a largish one of mixed breed. I leave it to you to judge what we had it for. I did not fire, nor did any of my party that I knew of. I heard two guns fired. Lord Stamford's preserves are pretty good ones.

He then old the court that they went towards Mr Egerton's plantation: only four of the keepers' party followed them there. None of them had gun or dog with them. They came up to the poachers at the River Bicken. Mr Yarwood knew Joseph Fenna, and came close to him – he was amongst ten or so others. Fenna was the last man, and said to Yarwood, 'Art thou measured for thy coffin? If thou dost not turn back I'll shoot thee,' pointing a gun toward Yarwood, but did not fire. Yarwood went on to say that the poachers' party then ran away, but were overtaken, and more than one of them said, 'D**n thy eyes, a'nt thee going back?', then the keepers saw a flash from several guns, but none of them went off. They pursued again, and came up to the party again, when several voices said 'Shoot! Shoot!' and one said, 'If thou don't, give me the gun and I will!' and the gun was passed from one to another. The four men from the keepers' party then retreated back some distance. The parties were on different sides of the hedge, and the poachers fired through a gap in the hedge. At the second shot Foster (a keeper) was hit. The court was told he exclaimed, 'Oh dear, they have broken my arm.'

There was a third shot, and the wadding of the gun came close to Mr Yarwood, who estimated it passed him by 20 or 30 yards. Foster was bleeding badly, and said that he thought he would die. The party then gave up the pursuit to carry Foster home, though a few followed the poachers to try and identify them.

Mr Yarwood said that only one shot had been fired by the gamekeepers. They had come up to the poachers many times. The poachers could have shot them, but Yarwood believed that they merely wanted to warn them off. 'We did not want to have any battle with them. If we had got hold of them we would not have let them go, I warrant you we pursued them for three miles.'

Mr Yarwood denied receiving any inducement from his employer to give evidence. He said he had received £2 compensation from Lord Stamford, for the injury to his arm and damage to his coat. Other injured keepers had also been given compensation. Mr Yarwood said he was the blacksmith to Lord Stamford at Dunham Massey, and was solely employed by him.

Mr Richard Winckley, another assistant keeper, gave corroborating evidence. He thought that when Foster was shot, the poachers were about 20 yards from them. Three shots were fired by the poachers. The first shot hit Clowes in the eye. Mr Sant, a keeper, returned fire, firing once.

He believed that the poachers snapped their guns to frighten them – the poachers had many opportunities to shoot them, if they had been so minded.

Leaflets were printed, offering the following rewards:

For these men a sum of £20 per head; Thomas Bamford, aka Beresford of Hay Head, labourer; Thomas Hulbert, aka Hullinworth of Hale Barns, wheelwright; and Joseph Massey of Timperley labourer; and a sum of £10 a head for William Hewitt of Timperley, a labourer John Taylor also of Timperley, wheelwright, John Jones of Gatley, labourer, John Henshaw or Henshall, a labourer of Hey Head, and John Boyle, another labourer, from Hale Barns. Some had been seen in Tatton Park, others at Dunham Massey.

Edward Hesketh, deputy constable of Altrincham and bailiff for Lord Stamford, said that on the following morning, the 23rd, he went to Fenna's father's house with Mr Shaw, at about half past five in the morning. Joseph Fenna was there, wet with perspiration. His shoes were very muddy. Perkins (the first witness) was also there and appeared in a similar state. They had a gun that had been recently fired. Constable Hesketh produced a waistcoat, gun and a bludgeon. The latter two had been found in Fenna's bedroom. Also found was a dead sheep. Another sheep had been shot the night before – the shotgun pellets on both fleeces were similar, showing that the same weapon had been used. Fenna was indicted for firing at gamekeepers during a wild chase across the local countryside.

Perkins confessed to being part of the poachers' group. Fenna and Perkins were taken to Altrincham. The three went to a public house in the town. The constable did not drink with Perkins before he went to the magistrates. This meant that Perkins had not been bribed into making a statement, and was sober when he did speak.

Perkins was remanded from the 24th to the 26th, during which time he was at the public house. Hesketh saw him on Christmas Day, though in the 1830s Christmas was not such a great celebration as it later became. Thomas Bamford was then detained with Perkins. The men appeared at the local magistrates' court before the formidable Mr Trafford Trafford of Oughtibridge. Born in 1770, Mr Trafford Trafford had been an informer for the government during the riots and troubles after the Napoleonic wars. He was a fierce upholder of law and order, so the local papers were sure that the poachers not only deserved to hang but would surely do so. Joseph Fenna was sent for trial at Chester Assizes on a charge of shooting at and wounding Thomas Foster, the gamekeeper. The evidence at that trial for the cross-country chase has been given above. However, the crucial charge, the one that could hang the defendant, was that of shooting to kill at Mr Foster.

Thomas Foster, the victim, was the last witness. He stated that he was the assistant gamekeeper on the estate. He was one of the keepers' party, and was hit twice, in two separate firing incidents. The last gun of the first firing hit him on the left cheek; the shot did not penetrate. At the second firing he was hit by the second gun. The shot entered the back of his neck and came out at the front. His arm dropped and it was a month or five weeks before he could use it. The waistcoat was produced as evidence at court. He swore that the one produced was the one he wore that day. It had a bullet hole at the back of the neck.

Mr Richard Broadbent, a surgeon of Higher Town, Altrincham, attended Mr Foster on 23 December. He found Foster dangerously wounded, with two wounds on the left side of the neck, and Broadbent had no doubt that the bullet had recently gone through as the wound was still bleeding. If the bullet had struck him in a vital part, it would have killed him. He did not consider that he was out of danger for eight or ten days; at present he was incapable of working. Mr Broadbent confirmed that the waistcoat produced in court was the one he had given to the constable.

When called upon to say something for his defence, Fenna said he left it to his counsel.

The judge summed up for over two hours. If the jury had no doubt about the poachers' guilt, then they would fearlessly and conscientiously do their duty.

The trial had lasted for eight hours, but the jury retired for just over an hour before returning a verdict of 'Not Guilty'. The court was crowded in the extreme, and the result seemed to surprise many. The prisoner was ordered to be detained at Her Majesty's Pleasure whilst awaiting trial on other matters.

Chapter Three

<hr>

Baddely the Foumart, 1829

The Cheshire police force did not exist until 1 June 1829. In that month the magistrates of Cheshire were granted a private Parliamentary Bill to set up a police force. This meant they now had the power to appoint Special High Constables, with supporting Assistant Petty Constables, and to raise the monies to pay for them. This move was not accepted by many, including magistrates, who regarded the new police force as a continental innovation and a threat to civil liberties. Local petitions were organised against the proposed police force – many signed by the local criminal community. At this time Wirral was plagued by smugglers and wreckers, but the local magistrates, who could not prevent such crimes, were vociferous in their opposition to the proposal for a county police force.

When finally set up in 1829, the police force itself had little power, as each police division was almost independent. There was no central body, and no head to give it direction and leadership. So the local communities were left to fend for themselves, pretty much as before – particularly the poor communities, where public opinion took the place of imposed authority. If a person was a conventional member of the local society, on good terms with their neighbours, life was pleasant. However, if anyone fell foul of the community then life could be made unpleasant. Very unpleasant.

One such man who fell foul of his community was John Baddely of Hyde, near Stockport. At nearly 60 years of age, he was an old man in 1828. But he was still capable of defending himself, using a thick stick with a large knob at its head, if he needed a weapon. And, as the Chester Assizes heard at the Lent Session in 1829, Baddely had indeed been a hunted man.

Quite why he was hated by his neighbours was not explained at the trial. However, his neighbours called him a 'foumart', a dialect word for a polecat, an animal renowned for an evil temper and bad smell.

What was revealed to the court that convened on Wednesday, 15 April 1829, before the Hon. Thomas Jervis, the Attorney General, was a horrifying story. The defendant was Stephen Shand, 31, accused of murder and manslaughter; the main witness was James Dalton, of Manchester.

James Dalton spent the night of 11 October 1828 in Hyde. But on that night he was caught up in some strange events. He told the court that he had had to go out at midnight on an unspecified errand, despite it being a rather dark night. About a quarter mile from his house, Mr Dalton saw Baddely and a number of persons following him.

Baddely told Dalton, 'They've been calling me a foumart.' The prisoner took hold of the skirt of his coat and said, 'Foumart, foumart, how art thee!' Whilst someone held his coat, Baddely struck Shand on the forehead with a stick, and Shand went down heavily on his hands and knees. When he got up he displayed a wound on his forehead about an inch in diameter – the size of an old halfpenny. The wound was bleeding profusely, and Shand wiped the blood away with his handkerchief. The stick was displayed in court – it was a very robust and formidable weapon.

Baddely ran away, with Shand after him, overtaking him. Despite being very drunk, and having suffered a severe blow to the head, Shand was still capable of violence. Having reached his victim, he struck Baddely a heavy blow to the back of the head, which knocked him down. Once on the road, Shand kicked Baddely twice in the head and once on the side. Baddely shrieked, 'Murder! Stephen, that is thee, and I'll swear my life against thee.'

Shand replied, 'I'll give thee something to swear away my life for.' James Walker, one of the crowd, and another witness in court, said that he grabbed Shand and begged him to give over; as so far he had not hurt Shand badly, and neither should Baddely be hurt. Another man, Turner, picked Baddely up from the road, whereupon Baddely ran away. Walker chased after him and caught him up about a quarter of a mile up the road, at a place called Clough Gate, and begged him to go home as soon as he could. Shand – and a crowd of onlookers – caught up with the two men at Clough Gate.

With the crowd urging him on, Shand came up to Baddely – who had tried in vain to get into a nearby house – and hit him, whereupon Baddely fell near the steps of the door. According to one witness, Shand then 'tumbled twice upon him, with his knees on his belly – I cannot say whether purposely or not.' Hearing the commotion, the people inside the house opened the door – and promptly shut it, due to a hail of stones and dirt thrown at them by the crowd.

Baddely sat on the house steps nursing his wounds. Shand went away, and all seemed over. However, the crowd shouted, 'Now Stephen! Now Stephen!' Hearing the cry, Shand returned to finish the job. By then the drink had taken full effect. Shand was so intoxicated he could hardly stand. He still had the energy to kick Baddely twice in the side.

Poor Baddely did not die immediately. He died two days later, at about 2 p.m. Mr Lear, the surgeon, opened up the body. He found the intestines to be greatly inflamed. In fact, one of them had burst; such was the violence that he had endured. That injury, said the surgeon, had recently been inflicted and was the cause of death.

Shand denied being responsible for the fatal blow. Another witness said he had seen numerous persons kick the deceased. In fact, it had been something of a sport in Hyde to hunt down Mr Baddely. The crowd that had hunted him down, and which Mr

Dalton had seen near his house, was not the crowd that killed him. Another crowd had collected and followed Shand to Clough Lane, where the final blows were inflicted – some by the crowd itself. The mob had enthusiastically joined in the battering of Baddely.

The judge, Mr Justice Jervis, said the case was clearly one of aggravated manslaughter. He lamented that the brutal practice of hunting the unpopular should exist in a Christian country.

The jury did not need to discuss the matter. They immediately produced a verdict of manslaughter. Shand was sentenced to two years hard labour. Even though contemporary prisons were unpleasant places, it still seems a lenient sentence for such an appalling crime.

Chapter Four

⇒·◇·⇐

The Ashton-under-Lyne Murder, 1830

Cheshire used to be described as a teapot. The body of the county provided the actual pot, Wirral was the spout, and the north-east was the handle. This area is the Tame Valley. It is now part of the administrative county of Greater Manchester. The River Tame flows through Stalybridge, Hyde and down to Stockport, where it joins the River Goyt to form the Mersey.

The upper valleys cut through the Pennines. At the end of the eighteenth century, the rushing streams were used to power simple machinery in cotton mills, staffed by the impoverished local peasantry. Local wages were below those in Manchester, and remained so for many years. The coming of steam power destroyed many such mills, but the Tame Valley was near coal supplies, so steam mills soon started up. For over a century, from about 1800 to 1914, the area was a major centre of textile production.

The people in the industry were a hard lot. In the early years of the nineteenth century, bitter strikes led to lockouts, starvation and murder. The murder of a cotton spinner shocked the nation, and is the subject of this chapter. First, a little background detail about the war between unions and masters.

A cotton spinners' union was proposed in 1829, and faced great hostility from the masters. They threatened to cut by ten per cent the wages of any operative who did not renounce the union. This caused anger amongst many workers. On 1 April 1829, a meeting was held at the Assembly Rooms of the Norfolk Arms pub in Hyde. Around 700 men attended, far more than the building could hold. The floor collapsed and thirty people were killed. Despite the tragedy, the union continued. A strike was called, for union recognition and higher wages. The masters threw out anyone known to be a union member. In the winter of 1830 there was great hardship in the district, with some 20,000 people out of work in the whole area of South East Lancashire and North Cheshire. Some fifty-two mills were closed at the time, due to strikes and lockouts. However, the unemployed were peaceable. Hyde mills were still at work.

The scene of the murder: Apethorne Lane, Werneth. (Courtesy of Tameside Local Studies and Archives Centre)

The Ashtons had a reputation as good employers, at both the family mills, at Apethorne and Woodley Mill.

In the early evening of Monday, 3 January 1830, Mr Thomas Ashton jnr, aged 23, was shot by an unknown assailant. He was the youngest member of the Ashton cotton dynasty. Mr Ashton was making his way from the family's factory to home, when he received two shots in the chest. The bullets killed him immediately. From foot marks by a roadside hedge, it appeared that more than one person had taken part in the murder.

Further investigation produced more details of his last hours. Thomas Ashton had taken tea with his family, then left to look at the new mill they had built. The mill was about a third of a mile from the family home. He was found dead at 8 p.m. He was reckoned to have been dead for less than an hour when discovered. Nothing was stolen from his person.

In his body there was one entrance wound, two exit ones. The gun had been loaded with two lead balls, which separated inside Mr Ashton's body, so he was obviously shot at very close range. There was doubt about the motive for murder. The Ashton-under-Lyne men were on strike, and industrial relations were very bitter. But the Hyde people were not on strike. However, the cause of the Ashton-under-Lyne strike was the attempt by the local masters to reduce wages to the Hyde level, so there was considerable bitterness felt in Ashton-under-Lyne about the Hyde masters. The Ashton family were also fiercely anti-union. However, they made up for low wages with excellent (by then standards) working conditions and benefits.

The wage rate dispute concerned the rate for 1,000 hanks of yarn at 40 hanks to the pound, i.e. one pound of cotton was spun into 40 hanks of yarn. The higher the number, the finer the cotton. The Ashton-under-Lyne men wanted 4s 2d per unit, or 'four and tuppence a swing' as local people called it. The masters offered 3s 9d on the grounds that Hyde people were paid only 3s 5d per unit.

Any attempt to compromise on 4s per unit would be resisted by both sides, said observers, as both were too proud to accept anything other than their own demands. The whole Tame Valley was occupied by troops, which assisted the police. The local police force remained independent of the Cheshire country force. However, the local High Constable was able to swear in many Special Constables for the duration of the troubles. Many dozens in fact.

Thomas Ashton was considered to be a kindly man, well liked by the working people. He was not responsible for setting wage rates. Older brother James Ashton was usually the manager at Apethorne Mill, Thomas was responsible for Woodley Mill. On that day, Thomas was deputising for his brother at Apethorne. In the dark, the assassins may have taken him for his brother. At least, that was the rumour in Manchester.

The inquest took place one week later, at the Boy & Barrel pub in Hyde. Other details emerged. A family servant, Hannah Sidebotham, said that Thomas left the family home after tea, about 7.30 p.m., to go to the Apethorne Mill. Mr Ashton's bloodstained body was found by two men walking along the same dark lane later. They did not recognise him at first. One went for a doctor, the other to the Ashton House. About fifteen minutes later, a messenger came and asked for Mr Thomas Ashton. 'He's not in,' said the lady servant.

'I know,' said the man. 'I think he's lying in the lane, hurt.' The man went away, followed by two female servants, to pick up the body. Only a few minutes after leaving his home, Thomas was brought in dead.

James Andrews, the book keeper at Apethorne Mill, said that three men had been fired recently, two of them for being members of a union. However, none of the dismissed employees had uttered any threats against Mr Ashton or his family.

An employee of the factory, 9-year-old Martha Percival, was returning home from the mill at about 7 p.m. to her father's house at Gerrard's Hollow when she met three men near the gate which led to the Ashton residence. She remembered hearing one walking the way between an old factory and Swindell's house. This distance was later measured as 100 yards. It was the route Mr Ashton had to take on his way home. The men blocked her path, so Hannah had to walk between them. She was sure that one of the men was carrying a gun.

Stockport Road, Gee Cross, c. 1910. The large building at the end of the street is the Grapes Hotel. Thomas Ashton's inquest was held at the Boy & Barrel pub, on the right of the picture, in 1831. (Courtesy of Tameside Local Studies and Archives Centre)

Mr Samuel Heginbottom, founder of a local cotton dynasty. (Courtesy of Tameside Local Studies and Archives Centre)

Other witnesses gave statements, and a verdict was returned of 'Wilful Murder by Person or Persons Unknown'. A reward of £600 was offered to anyone who gave information leading to an arrest of the culprits. Other monies were soon added, making a total reward of £1,500 – a fortune at the time.

The authorities brought up two policemen from London. The Metropolitan's finest were Messrs Bishop and Ruthven. They did their best, but those who knew did not talk, and those who talked did not know. Two men were soon apprehended and the case was dismissed. A more credible case was made by a Mr Jones, who was in his late teens. Arrested on a charge of robbery, he spent his time in the cell pacing up and down, never sleeping or relaxing. On being asked why he behaved so strangely, he replied that he was consumed by guilt over the murder of Mr Ashton. He claimed the actual murderer had been a tailor named Mr Trotter. Jones gave some details about the murder. He said it had been planned in a pub. After the event, Trotter had given Jones 20 sovereigns as hush money.

Taken before the magistrates, Jones displayed strange behaviour. He grimaced, shook, and shivered with seemingly unbearable guilt. Upon further investigation, his story was proven to be an illusion – much to Mr Trotter's relief.

Meanwhile, the dispute dragged on and grew bitterer. For example, in June 1830, a stranger hired a young boy to take a packet to Mr Heginbottom of Ashton-under-Lyne. The wife of the house opened it to find a loaded pistol. To make sure of a murder, the packet also contained 'several pounds of the best gunpowder', which would have been ignited by the sparks from the gun. The workers were starved back to work at their old rates from February 1831. No more details of clues about the Ashton murder came to light. In fact it was to be almost three years before the real culprits came to court.

The breakthrough came from an informant. William Garside was serving 18 months detention in Derby Gaol on an unrelated matter. He had been imprisoned for stealing a spindle box from his employer. Witnesses said he acted peculiarly in his cell. He slept badly, and appeared preoccupied with something. Apparently, he had also read in the 'Hue and Cry' – a police journal – that the Ashton mystery was still unsolved. The article also said that there was a substantial reward still available to any informant. To him, this seemed an ideal way to get out of prison with some money. So, he called for the Governor of Derby Gaol, a Mr John Sims, and told him he had some information about the murder of Mr Ashton, but refused to say any more until he saw the Stockport magistrates. The Governor and the prison doctor, Dr Forrester, were also in the cell. Garside asked them if he would receive a pardon for his information.

They said they could not guarantee he would. Dr Forrester called for him to be taken off the treadmill and separated from the other prisoners. He must have given some details of the murder, including the names of two brothers, Joseph and William Mosley, because they were soon arrested. The Mosleys were the local bad lads, four brothers who were all involved in robberies and assaults. Joseph became a fortune teller, and made a good living touring the countryside telling fortunes.

Back in Derby, Garside again requested to see the magistrate, Mr William Jeffery Lockett, the visiting magistrate for Derby Gaol. He was brought up to the Governor's office. The first thing he did was to ask if Joseph Mosley was in custody. The second question, 'Would I be made a Crown witness?' Mr Lockett said he thought it likely that Mosley was in custody. However, he could give no guarantees about witness protection. That decision was in the hands of the Court. Garside seemed willing to give more information. Lockett told him that if he gave more information, it would not guarantee that he would be made a Crown witness and given a pardon.

Garside was about to make a statement when Lockett said, 'Stop it! Let us see what is in "Hue and Cry"' and asked the turnkey to fetch a copy. Perusing the paper, Lockett saw there was no mention of a pardon for the actual murderer. He read the relevant piece to Garside.

Garside was very agitated, and asked, 'Can I be made a witness without a pardon? Lockett said 'Pardon for which crime? The one for which you are now imprisoned?' Garside said 'Yes', but Lockett gave no reply.

Lockett later returned with Mr James Ashton to see Garside, who said very little of substance, but he did ask Mr Lockett about the prospects for a reward and pardon. To his credit, Mr Lockett made no promises. Or so he told the court.

Back in Cheshire, the Deputy Constable of Stockport, Mr John Stavely Barratt of Vernon Street Stockport, had arrested Joseph Mosley. Joseph was on his way from Chester to Liverpool at the time. He denied all knowledge of the Ashton murder, except for what he had heard in the locality at the time.

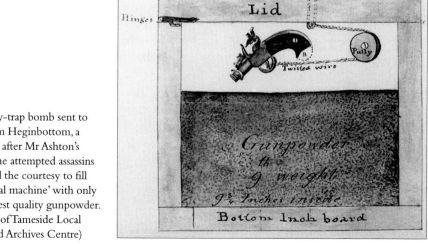

The booby-trap bomb sent to Mr William Heginbottom, a few weeks after Mr Ashton's murder. The attempted assassins at least had the courtesy to fill the 'infernal machine' with only the very best quality gunpowder. (Courtesy of Tameside Local Studies and Archives Centre)

The trial took place in 1834, at the Summer Assizes in Chester Castle. Two men were tried; Joseph Mosley (34), and William Garside. William Garside was defended by a Mr Dunn, whilst Joseph Mosley defended himself.

William Mosley, brother of Joseph, gave evidence against his brother and Garside. William claimed that they had fired the fatal shot. He, his brother and Garside had agreed to carry out the murder at the suggestion of Samuel Scholefield, an official of the Cotton Spinners' Union. For successful completion of the deed, they were to get £10 between them, or 3 guineas each.

He told the court more details. William said he had been a boat man, who lived at Romiley, about a mile and a half from Mr Ashton's house and four miles from Marple. He knew Garside from Marple. On the evening of Wednesday, 29 December 1830, he met his brother and Garside at the Stag's Head pub in Marple Bridge. Over a drink he told them about his woes. He was unemployed, and preparing to go to Macclesfield to seek work. Garside said that if he stopped in the area for a few days, he might be given work that would pay better than any other job he could find in Macclesfield. At that suggestion William perked up, and promised to meet them again on the Sunday at Marple Bridge.

That he did, meeting them on the bridge. They discussed things for a half hour between noon and one. William was told that they were all going to nearby Compstall Brow, where he was to be introduced to two men who would provide employment.

William knew both of the men by sight. One was a joiner, named Scholefield or Stanfield. Joseph told his brother to stand aside whilst he talked with the two men. William did not hear much of the conversation, but in the half hour they talked, he did hear 'the Unions' mentioned. After the conversation, the two men went away. Garside and Joseph Moseley told William that they had agreed with the two men that they were to shoot one of the Ashtons. William asked, 'What for?'

'Because of the turn out of the unions' was the reply.

'What do we get out of it?'

'Ten pounds.'

William was told to meet his brother and Garside the next day for the murder. The rendezvous was to be either Wrights Tower or the gravel pits. William demurred, but was persuaded to join in the conspiracy. So, the next day at 4 p.m. he set out from Romiley to Wrights Tower, and missed them. Going on to the Gravel Pit, he met them. Both men had loaded pistols. Garside's pistol was large 'Like a horse pistol' (these were large pistols used by cavalrymen to shoot enemy horses) and the other had a small gun with a bright barrel.

Clothes and shoes were swapped, to prevent recognition. They passed some people on the way, including a little girl. They came to the appointed place. When they saw a man approaching, both Garside and Mosley fired their guns at him. The victim was about 20 yards from the Clap Gate when hit. Once the shot had been fired the assassins fled. William asked which of the Ashtons had been shot. 'It doesn't matter – it was one of them.'

William was 'appointed' to meet the other two at the Bull's Head in Marple the next day. After sleeping the night on a friend's boat, he went to the Bull's Head. There he met his brother, Garside and the union man, Scholefield or Stanfield. The man said he had settled with the other two, and would now give William his share. He drew three sovereigns from his pocket, but William said he would be glad of only two. All the men signed a book, William with his mark – he was illiterate.

Then they all went down on their knees, and held a knife, one over the other, swearing an oath, 'May God strike us dead if we ever tell.'

William Mosley told the trial that he had kept his secret until May 1834. He had been held at Knutsford Gaol on a charge of stealing a spade. He had never been in any other prison. He told his story a few days after being arrested on 8 April 1834, and was held at Stockport until 7 May. In cross-examination, it was revealed that what he said in court differed from what he had originally told the magistrates, and what the other defendants said. Nonetheless, he agreed to stand witness against his brother and James Garside. At the trial, questions were asked of Mr Barratt's conduct. In particular – had he bribed William Mosley? Both men denied the accusation. William said he had been given monies by Barratt, but that it was his own money that Barratt was transferring to him, to buy tobacco.

At the trial, Garside said that Dr Forrester had promised that he would get not only a pardon for his present sentence, but for the murder also, and a share of the reward to boot. Garside also said that Dr Forrester had been deliberately kept away from the trial so that he could not testify to the truth of the promise. Garside claimed that Mr Sims, the Governor, had made similar promises. Mr Sims was in the court and flatly denied making any such promise.

Joseph Mosley made his own written defence. He claimed that he was innocent of any crime, blaming his brother William and Garside, not only for the murder but for many other crimes. In fact, Joseph claimed that Garside and William were the sort who would swear away a man's life for a drink.

One defence witness was a fellow prisoner named Enoch Bradley. He had been in the prison hospital with William Mosley. Bradley said William Mosley had been badly treated by Barratt. William had been put into the condemned cell at Chester Castle on arrival, and told he would stay there until the Assizes, unless he told all. Bradley also stated that William boasted of getting a share of the reward money following the execution, and £20 from Barratt's own pocket.

Both William Mosley and Barratt denied all Bradley's charges. In fact, everything Bradley (a thief) had said was totally untrue. Mr John Dunstan, Governor of Chester Castle, said that William had been put in the condemned cell to keep him separate from the other prisoners, and moved to alternative accommodation as soon as possible.

The trial went on all day. The judge allowed the jury a few minutes respite just after 9 p.m. They could leave whilst the judge prepared his summing up. One of the jury went into a nearby pub to have a refreshing rum and water at Mr Parry's spirit vaults. The landlord had been in court, recognised the juror, and told him to get back quick, as the case had not ended, but was about to begin again. At 9.30 p.m. the juror returned to the jury box and the summing up began after a reprimand to the miscreant juror.

After a few minutes discussion they returned a verdict of 'Guilty' on the defendants, who both promptly fainted, whilst 'several females in the court also sobbed aloud'.

The next step was to decide which of the two men had fired the fatal shot. To encourage the tired jurors, the judge put them in a room with only a candle for light. They were told they would be kept there without food or drink until a verdict was reached. A verdict came quickly – Garside was the one who had fired the shot.

The judge, Mr Baron Parke, passed sentence of death, explaining that he could give the prisoners no false hopes of mercy. They had forty-eight hours to live. In fact they were to live a little longer, as numerous petitions and legal arguments followed the verdict.

A legal row started between the county and City of Chester. Previously, the county authorities, the High Sheriff of Cheshire, handed over prisoners from Chester Castle to the High Sheriff of Chester City. Prisoners were then hung from the walls of the City Gaol. However, a recent change in the law led the city authorities to declare that they were now under now obligation to hang the condemned men. So they refused to hang Mosley and Garside.

Baron Parke gave the men ten days respite. The dispute dragged on. Taking advantage of the 'respite', the lawyers of the condemned men argued for a reprieve on the grounds that both men had informed to the authorities. They had blamed each other for the fatal shot. Hanging them, certainly hanging Joseph Mosley, would discourage others from informing. At a time when the undermanned police force relied upon informers, that was a powerful argument.

Eventually, both men were taken to London and kept at the King's Bench Prison awaiting either execution or reprieve. Joseph Mosley acted 'with great decency', expecting a reprieve right up until the last moment. The night before the execution, their wives were allowed a first and final visit. The women had followed their men down from Chester, as had the Stockport High Constable. Mosley met Mr Barratt and other officials, giving Barratt a slip of paper on which were more details of his crime.

The two were sent to Horsemonger Lane Gaol for their final night. At 5 o'clock on the morning of Tuesday, 25 November 1834, they were hung from the gates of the prison before the usual appreciative crowd.

The authorities arrested the union man, Mr Schofield, but the case fell through due to the lack of solid evidence. As for the Ashtons, the family continued to rise in wealth and fame. They remained progressive and popular employers. A grandson later became Liberal MP for the town.

Chapter Five

⟸⬦⟹

The Union Martyrs Who Escaped, 1834

The Tolpuddle Martyrs were a group of Dorset labourers who were transported to Australia in 1834 for trying to form a trade union. Trade unions had been made illegal under the Combination Acts, repealed in the 1820s. However, repeal of the law did not give much legal protection to unions or friendly societies. An official of a society could take away the funds of the union, savings club, burial society or whatever. As non-legal entities, the society could not take legal action as a group. The other members would have to take out individual actions against the miscreant.

So, to prevent their funds being swindled or stolen, most unions and societies made their officials and members swear bloodcurdling oaths, with graphic descriptions of the terrible pain which would be inflicted upon anyone who broke the society's rules. However, the swearing of such oaths was illegal, and, following a local lawyer's discovery of the 1797 Mutiny Act against swearing oaths, the Tolpuddle Martyrs were sentenced for swearing illegal oaths. Their trial was held in March 1834.

Following the trial, Mr William Lowe, a Nantwich solicitor, read about the events and thought that similar action could be taken against some society men then in dispute at the premises of Richard Walker, shoe manufacturer. Walker employed one William Cappur, described by John Dunning, a prominent activist, as a 'halfwit'. This young man was persuaded to tell Walker and Lowe the names of those who had initiated him into the union. By administering illegal oaths, the shoemaker's union men had broken the law.

In later life John Dunning wrote a detailed account of his activities. In particular, he told how he and his colleagues managed to avoid the fate of the Dorset men.

Nantwich is now a prosperous and very conservative town. In the 1830s, the poor were poor. Shoemakers earned about 9s for a week of twelve to sixteen-hour days, roughly the same as the local farm labourers. In Dorset, the Tolpuddle men were trying to get 10s a week, when local rates were 7s a week, and these rates being further cut to 6s a week.

Shoemakers' poverty has already been mentioned, but their poverty did not preclude an interest in politics. Shoemakers enjoyed political arguments and strong liquor. Shoemaking was a trade taught in prisons, as it was easy to learn, though it required nimble fingers. These dexterous digits were also useful in less respectable trades. A high proportion of pickpockets were, or had been, shoemakers.

Shoemakers supported the Great Reform Bill of 1832. The Nantwich men clubbed together to buy the *Weekly Dispatch*, the leading radical newspaper of the day. One member of this club was the Unitarian minister, the Revd James Hawkes. Dunning's memoir hints that trade associations existed even then in Nantwich, because he says that after the 1832 Reform Bill they amalgamated to form a shoemakers' union, roughly 500 strong. They paid subscription fees to a national organisation, believed to have been the Operative Cordwainers, a founder organisation of the Grand National Consolidated Trades Union. After fee payments they had about £40 left over, and, not knowing what better to do with it, they purchased a banner (£25) and spent the rest on a full set of secret order regalia, surplices, trimmed aprons etc., which were proudly displayed in procession through Nantwich on the next St Crispin's Day, 25 October, 1833. A deputation was sent to ask the Revd Gratton to bless the procession.

The local Anglican vicar, however, declined to bless the procession unless he could read the rules of the organisation, which were secret, so the request was refused. They knew the Wesleyans were opposed to trade societies, and therefore considered it useless to solicit them for chapel and sermon.

The volunteered services of the Revd Hawkes were gratefully accepted. A grand parade went through the town, with a 'King Crispin on horseback at the front', (Saints Crispin and Crispian were two brothers, shoemakers, martyred for their Christian beliefs). Dunning said that nearly 500 people joined the procession, neatly attired in white aprons. Clearly, they presented a threat to the master shoemakers and merchants – hence the desire to smash the union.

At the time of Cappur's arrest in April 1834, Dunning lodged with Mrs Cooke and her two sons, Benjamin (the Treasurer of the union) and Samuel (the Tramping President of the union). News had spread rapidly and they all expected immediate arrest following Cappur's apostasy. They saw Constable Pritchard enter the home of Matthew Bayley, another society officer. Bayley was 'a light minded, dancing, public house sort of man' who was 'barely literate'. Dunning went to Bayley's house across the road from his lodgings, engaged in banter with Pritchard, and returned across the road to find the Cookes had fled, leaving behind regalia, cash and society records. The Cookes were on their way to Manchester. Perhaps a wise decision. That evening, Matthew Bayley and Richard Blagg were arrested on warrants charging them with administering illegal oaths. They were sent to the town lock-up, known as the 'Round House', on Snow Hill.

The arrests caused great excitement as nearly every working man's family was connected to the shoe trade. A small meeting decided to call upon Mr Thomas W. Jones, the lawyer. They did not know if he was in Chester, as the Assizes had just started, or at his home in Hough. Dunning and others went to Hough, and found Mr Jones at home. He told them he would not appear in court with the prisoners. Since his victory in the Darnhall Hall affair (in which he had had a poachers' case quashed

The frontage of the former Lamb Hotel, now the Chadderton Buildings. This building was erected in the 1860s to replace the old Lamb Hotel. Both old and new buildings served many functions in local government and postal services. Today it is an apartment and business development.

because a legal document had not specified whether the incident in question took place at 12 noon or 12 midnight), he had not been popular with the magistrates. His appearance in court could prejudice the case against them. He told the deputation to get the message to the men that they must say nothing. The men on remand could have meals sent in to them, so the next morning Mrs Bayley and Mrs Blagg took in breakfast rolls; they had been told to tell their husbands the legal advice. There was also a note inside each roll giving Mr Jones's advice.

While this was going on, Dunning made arrangements to remove the main witness, William Cappur. Dunning met Cappur at his home and promised him work and lodgings in Manchester. Another shoemaker, a Mr Wilkinson, known to Cappur, was going to Manchester the next morning. Wilkinson was to ask the coach to stop, pick up Cappur and pay his fare. Cappur agreed immediately. His parents were pleased to have him leave the town and its unpleasantness.

However, Richard Wilkinson knew nothing of the plot. Dunning went to him and, as he hoped, Wilkinson agreed to the plan, so next morning Cappur was on his way to Manchester, where the local shoemakers would keep him safe.

However, as many local men either worked in Manchester or went to the weekly shoe market there, he was in danger of being recognised, so the union paid for him to go to Dublin. They had to pay for his upkeep as he was a 'very inferior workman'. The cash could not be sent from Nantwich post office as that was at the Lamb Hotel, the watering hole of the local Tories. Dunning walked the 20 miles to Chester every so often to send the cash from there.

The two imprisoned men were bailed pending trial at the Assizes in Chester. So they returned to Nantwich, accompanied by John Dunning. On the way back, a few people met them to shake hands and give congratulations about six miles from Nantwich. At every mile, the welcoming crowds grew larger. When they arrived in the town, the crowds were so large Dunning could hardly drive along the streets.

The case was called in April 1835. It turned out to be the last case of the sessions. The crier of the court called out several times, 'William Cappur, come forward, or your recognizances will be forfeited.' But no Cappur appeared. Constable Pritchard went into the witness box and swore on oath that the Unionists had taken the witness away, but that the witness would appear in time for the next Assizes. With that statement, the case collapsed.

Meanwhile, poor Cappur was taken ill with measles. The Nantwich men were afraid he would die. If so, his family and the authorities would suspect that he had been murdered. Money was sent to him to pay for his care, and he recovered.

The next Assizes also lasted a week and, as before, the Nantwich case was the last to be dealt with. As Cappur did not appear, Superintendent Pritchard could not swear to deliver the chief witness. So again the case collapsed, and both Bayley and Blagg were released. There was great rejoicing in Nantwich.

Cappur reappeared in Nantwich about two years later, claiming to have no memory of where he had been at the crucial time. His father, a gamekeeper at Wistaston Hall, was sacked by his employer, James Hammond Esq.; 'a Tory of the first water' who suspected Cappur Senior of knowing his son's whereabouts.

So, the Nantwich shoemakers escaped the fate of the Dorset labourers. But the employers had won a victory. The affair virtually bankrupted the society, as legal costs alone amounted to £80, without counting the monies paid to families of the men who fled. It was all paid off, though the society reverted to simple Cordwainers Club. The returning shoemakers scoffed at the expense incurred as 'too great'. This disgusted the men who had borne the burden and heat of the day, many of whom took no interest in the society afterwards. The unions remained neutered until the late 1850s, when the town was racked by strikes over the introduction of new machinery into the shoemaking trade.

Dunning was not discouraged. He was interested in music and politics; in 1837 he played in the town band to celebrate Queen Victoria's Coronation. He became active in the Chartist movement. When that collapsed, he continued his activities in local affairs. He worked as a newsagent until his death in 1894.

Chapter Six

⇒◇⇐

The Peover Murder, 1840

In the summer of 1840, the county was shocked by the barbarous murders of two respectable old folk. They were retired farmer Mr Cook, who was 70 years old, and his wife, who was a semi-invalid. Mr Cook had been a farmer for forty years and was a tenant of the Mainwaring family. He lived on his savings and rents from letting land. He was still hale and stout, despite his age.

The culprit was eventually tracked down to Ireland, thanks to two scraps of paper found at the murder scene.

The murders took place in the quiet settlement of Peover, about two miles from Knutsford, on the 'green lane' around the park of Sir Harry Mainwaring. The lane formed part of the route between Knutsford and Macclesfield.

On this lane was a two-storied house of four bedrooms above, and four rooms below, which were three rooms and a scullery. In this house lived Mr and Mrs Cook, the victims, and their servant girl, Rebecca Morgan, about 15 years of age.

She came into the Cooks' service the Christmas before, i.e. December 1839, and lived quietly with the old couple. That August night, Monday 24th, Rebecca later said, their neighbour Mr Lea (spelt Lear in some accounts) supped with them. After the meal Mr Cook went to bed at half past eight, as did Rebecca. Mrs Cook stayed up to wash and bandage her feet. She came to the bedroom, and stayed talking to her husband. Rebecca was awake in her room when the clock struck ten. A little time after that she heard a crashing sound, which she thought was mugs breaking. She heard Mrs Cook shout, 'Joseph, can't you get a light?' Rebecca heard no reply. Mrs Cook went downstairs. Rebecca heard her say 'Oh Lord!' That shout was followed a few minutes later by a sound like somebody falling, accompanied by Mrs Cook's cry of 'Oh Murder!' and no more sounds were heard.

A few moments later, Rebecca was terrified to see a man in her room. She was still in bed, and made no noise. She saw the man stand by the bed, on the side near the window. By the light from the window, she could see that he was a tall man, and she thought that he was dressed in dark clothes. He looked towards her, but then left the

These cottages give some idea of what Knutsford was like in the early nineteenth century. They are at the end of King Street, near the Tatton Hall entrance.

bedroom and went into the old couple's bedroom. There was a smashing, crunching sound, as of someone breaking open the cupboard door. Then Rebecca heard the man go downstairs. She remained in bed, paralysed with fear, hearing the clock strike the hours eleven, twelve, one, until three. She did not hear the four o'clock chime. She did hear the five o'clock chime, at which she awoke. She came downstairs to a terrible sight – her employer and his wife lay battered and dead on the floor. Grabbing her shoes and bonnet in her hands, she fled the scene to give the alarm to the neighbours. Leaving by the back door, she went to the house of Mr Lea, not only a neighbour but the brother-in-law of Mr Cook. He sent Rebecca to fetch the local constable, whilst he himself went to the cottage. On the way he met a dishevelled man, a rough sleeper whose clothes were still spotted with straw. He took the man with him as a witness, and went to the murder scene. Rebecca had met the local constable, Mr John Kinder, who came back with her to the cottage. They came into the house to see a horrific sight. On the kitchen floor lay the bloodied bodies of Mr and Mrs Cook. They had obviously been in bed before they got up and went downstairs: he was dressed only in his nightclothes, namely his trousers and waistcoat, while she was in a nightgown. Mrs Cook's body was nearest to the door; Mr Cook's body was in the far corner of the room. Around both was a stream of dried blood. Both had been battered with an axe, which had split their skulls open. The bloodstained axe was lying on the table. It was recognised by Rebecca, who identified it as one owned by Mr Cook, and usually kept in the shippon (cowshed) adjoining the property.

The witnesses were joined at 7 a.m. by PC John Topham. Mr Lea had been joined by Miss Lea. Mr Lea, Mr Harding (the rough sleeper) and PC Topham gingerly stepped around the bodies to search for any evidence. By the candlestick they found two pieces of paper. Though ripped and burnt, as if torn up to light the candle, they still bore some legible writing. The words revealed were testimonials, a character, as the Victorians called it. In short, a 'to whom it may concern' letter, recommending the reader to employ the paper's holder. One was in blue ink, the other in black. On one was later found the name and address of a Mr Plunkett of Cavan, the other Mr McNally of Ballyconnell.

This pretty little alleyway, almost unaltered for centuries, is just off King Street in Knutsford.

The surgeon of Knutsford, Mr Dean, examined the bodies and came to the obvious conclusion that the couple had been killed by the axe. However, their deaths had been almost instantaneous. The bodies were left in the house until the visit of the coroner's jury that afternoon. The inquest itself was held at the Mainwaring Arms public house, before the local coroner, Mr Hollins. News of the murders had spread throughout the district, and dozens of locals were gathering in the area around the murder scene.

The hastily-assembled court heard evidence from Mr Dean, Rebecca, Mr Lea, and Mr Harding, the rough sleeper. He was an unemployed wheelwright from nearby Goostrey, returning from Manchester, where he had gone 'on the tramp' to seek work.

Not finding any employment, he had started to walk home. Exhausted before he reached Goostrey, he decided to sleep rough at a convenient spot. He had slept by the side of a haystack, near to the Cooks' cottage.

He told the assembly that he had heard the cottage door open, a sound like crashing crockery, then sounds of a row, followed by what he thought was a girl's voice saying, 'Don't master', then silence. He thought that the master of the house had chastised a servant for breaking crockery, and thought no more about it. He heard no more noise and went to sleep. At the break of day he awoke, and was walking home when he met Mr Lea. The two men's accounts of what followed tallied. Hearing all the limited evidence available, the coroner's jury returned a verdict of 'Wilful murder by person or persons unknown'.

Mr Harper, Special High Constable of the District, led a search of the cottage. Mr William Harper had come to Cheshire from the Metropolitan Police. He was one of three Special High Constables who had responsibility for Cheshire. Under him, Harper had only eight Petty Constables. However, they were very conscientious and energetic, and got results. Harper and his team came to the conclusion that Mr Cook must have been attacked by at least two people, and that he knew one or both of them. He was known to be very particular about not letting in strangers late at night. To keep intruders at bay, he kept what Rebecca said was an 'angry dog'. The dog always barked noisily at strangers. She had not heard it bark that night. Footprints had been found in the damp ground by the garden walk, and through the border hedge. An iron candlestick was also found, Mr Cook's own, but at first sight there was little missing from the cottage. A desk had been broken open in the murder room, but a silver plate and other valuables in cupboards had not been touched.

A bag, identical to one owned by Mr Cook, was found thrown away in a nearby churchyard. It was later confirmed to be Mr Cook's.

Mr Harper and his police force became very active and found witnesses. Mr Robinson of Peover said he rented land from Mr Cook. He had paid his rent – 14 guineas – to Mr Cook a day or so before the murder. Mr Cook had put the money into a bag – the very bag found in the churchyard of Knutsford parish church. Mr Robinson had seen the bag last when Mr Cook put the money-filled bag into his cupboard. The very cupboard that had been smashed open on Monday night.

Suspicion fell on the local Irish labourers hired for the harvest. That was partly because of prejudice. Victorian Britain was bitterly anti-Catholic and anti-Irish. There was a more substantial reason for suspicion – the

Knutsford parish church, where the bag was found.

two scraps of paper giving a 'character' to an unknown Irishman. Asking questions amongst the harvester community, the police found that one young Irishman, 18-year-old Benjamin Murray, had left the area quickly following the murder. The fair-haired Murray was a good-looking young man.

Two Irish harvesters, James and William Fitzpatrick, had worked with Murray the Saturday before the murder, at Prescot (near Widnes). The Fitzpatricks confirmed that Murray was then absolutely penniless. He told them that he was returning to Knutsford to pick up a bag of belongings.

He was seen near Mr Cook's cottage around 12 noon on the day of the murder, Monday. The people working on Mr Ditchfield's farm provided that information. Mr Ditchfield's farm was near to the Cooks' house. The cottage could be seen from the field being harvested. Samuel Rees, the farmer's lad, said that Murray had seen the Cooks' cottage, and asked if they were rich. Rees replied, 'Yes, very.' Another employee of Mr Ditchfield was 'shearing' the wheat in the field that day. Breaking for a meal, he was going along the lane to the farmhouse to eat. On the way he met Murray, who asked if there was any work available. He said there was none available, and saw Murray walk away towards the Cooks' cottage.

Two women, Mrs Foden and Mrs Snelson, said they had seen Murray that Monday afternoon near to the Cooks' cottage.

Another witness was Mr William Evison, an estate steward. At 9.30 p.m. on the evening of the murder, he had left work late and was leading his horse along the lane near the Cooks' cottage when he heard the chimes of 10 o'clock. He saw someone in dark clothes run past him, towards Knutsford.

Mr Terence 'Teddy' Riley, Irish landlord of a lodging house at Bowling Green Knutsford, confirmed that Murray had stayed from Sunday afternoon until Tuesday morning. On the Monday night, he went to bed at 10 o'clock by his clock – but it was an unreliable wooden one. The Rileys ran it fast, to ensure that they would wake in time in the morning. Mrs Hannah Riley stayed awake. She saw Murray come in, at a time – by their wooden clock – of 10.15 p.m. Most lodgers came in much earlier – it was very unusual for them to come in so late. She asked him why he was so late. He said that he had been walking from his work, about 6-7 miles away. She asked him why he had not just slept rough for the night.

'They did not have a barn with enough straw to make a comfortable bed,' he replied. So saying, he went to bed. He said he would not be returning to his workplace the next morning. She offered him a light to illuminate his way in the dark house, but he refused the offer. He said later that he knew Mrs Riley was ill, and did not want to trouble her for a candle. He knew his way, as he had often gone to bed without a light before. The next day, Tuesday, he was gone before the Rileys woke up. When he left he was wearing his usual clothes. These were a dark brown coat with bright buttons over a pair of grey trousers.

On that Tuesday, 25 August, as the bodies were being discovered in Knutsford, Murray walked to the railway station and bought a ticket to Liverpool where he bought new clothes: an engineer's suit and 'Jim Crow' hat, plus a ticket to Dublin on a cattle boat. The boat left for Ireland on Wednesday, the 26th, and he reached his native Cavan on Thursday the 27th, by stage car. He did not stay there long.

He was arrested and taken to the Irish capital, then from Dublin by post packet on Saturday night, 5 September, in the custody of Mr Harper, who had arrested him in Cavan. They arrived in Liverpool early Sunday morning, and promptly went to the Knutsford House of Correction at 1 p.m.

The next morning began a series of preliminary investigations under the senior magistrate Mr Trafford Trafford. Mr Trafford Trafford was very much a magistrate of the old school – he may even have been a Home Office informer during the troubled years after the Napoleonic Wars. Over the next few days, the magistrates' court heard the following details.

Mr James Atherton of Latchford, near Warrington, said that the Sunday before the murder, Murray had come to his beer house and enquired about trains. Specifically, train times to Liverpool from Warrington at night. He was told that a train went 5 p.m. that very afternoon. Murray said he was not going to Liverpool that night, but to Knutsford. A few days later, on the Tuesday, Murray returned to the station to eat and await a train. James Highland, an Irishman, had worked with Murray, and said that he had seen Murray's 'characters' and identified them as being signed by Mr Plunkett and Mr Halpen. He had not seen the papers open, but when Murray had shown them to an employer, he could see that one was in black ink, the other in blue. Murray had also borrowed 1s 6d from him and not repaid it – when asked he always claimed to have no money.

Other witnesses came from Liverpool and Ireland. Mr Harper, the senior constable, had been busy in Ireland finding witnesses.

Shopkeepers from Liverpool said that Murray had bought a suit for 17s and shoes for 7s 6d. A Dublin lodging house keeper, Mr John Lamb, who was also a schoolmaster, stated that he hired a room to a lodger. He identified him as Murray, and said the young man had desired to hire a cart to Cavan. Mr Lamb had said that a cart was going to Cavan the next day. Mr Lamb knew the driver, and hailed him as the cart was passing the lodging house. Murray took with him to Cavan a trunk containing hardware – another witness said that Murray had purchased many articles of hardware that Wednesday morning, 26 August. A large amount, up to £6 worth, paid for in cash, sovereigns and silver.

The cart driver, Thomas Farley stated that he picked up Murray outside Lamb's lodging house and took him to Cavan. Murray left the cart about a mile and a half before they reached the town. On the way he had paid 6s for the trip, plus a 6d tip and a round of whisky for the other passengers.

Other witnesses gave their statements. One especially interesting one was that of Henry Savill, a gentleman's servant, who lent him 7s on Saturday 2 August. Security for the loan was provided by a pawn ticket for a watch, in the name of William Fitzpatrick, which Murray claimed was his name.

Mrs Ellen Buckle, the widow who ran the Mainwaring Arms in Lower Peover, said that she had seen Murray many times. On the murder day, he was outside at noon, and later she was sure that she had seen him with another man at sometime between 8 p.m. and 9 p.m. She heard one ask, 'What shall we do if she comes?' and the other replied, 'D**n her, serve her the same.'

Mr Evison, the steward of Toft Hall stables, repeated his evidence of seeing someone run past him. This was confirmed by his wife, who said that she had seen a young man 'about the size of the prisoner' run past her house.

Mr Harper, the Special High Constable for the Hundred of Bucklow, gave his evidence, as above. The proceedings took six hours, during which Murray was seated in a chair. His demeanour remained calm and resolute throughout the day.

The prisoner was asked if he had anything to say in his defence.

He calmly replied 'No, Sir.' He was then told that he was to be committed to trial at the next Assizes in Chester. Mr Harper was appointed to be the prosecutor.

The trial took place in Chester at the Spring Assizes of 1841. The court was packed for the proceedings, which took place on Tuesday 13 April. Murray's defence was paid for by his uncle, who arrived for Ireland to support his nephew. Murray was found guilty. Observers noted his remarkably calm and poised manner, despite his young age – 19 when condemned – and the serious matter of the case.

However, there were strange aspects to the case. No blood was ever found on his clothes or possessions. Mr Dean, the surgeon of Knutsford, stated that the blood might not have spurted upon the killer. If that opinion was correct, then the absence of blood did not clear Murray.

No possession of the Cooks was ever found in his possession, apart from money, which by its nature was not traceable to any one individual. No confession was ever made, though a fellow prisoner, Mr Coates, said he had heard such a confession. Coates' character was not such as to inspire confidence, so his evidence was never given to the open court. Murray's defence lawyer had questioned Mr Harding's activities on the night, asking why he had not entered the house when he heard the disturbance inside. That attempt to divert attention failed.

Murray's case was not helped by the lack of defence witnesses. No one gave him an alibi. Forty-six other witnesses gave evidence as to his rapid getaway on the Tuesday. If he had worked with an accomplice, as the police first suspected, he never gave away the name.

He took his death sentence with the same calm that he had displayed throughout. When asked for his comments, he said, 'Gentlemen, I'm as innocent as a child unborn, and it's not right that I should suffer for others.'

Later, he became very depressed. Newspaper reports said he was receiving great comfort from the Catholic chaplain. He was kept in the castle.

He was executed on the morning of Saturday 26 April, just under two weeks after the trial. Until the Thursday night before the execution, he had retained his usual calm composure. The Friday morning he received the Holy Sacrament, administered by the Revd J. Carberry. Murray fell into depression, and took an interest in religion. He still retained his good manners – he shook hands with another prisoner, suspected of shooting at a gamekeeper; he wished him good luck and an escape from the fate which was to befall him. He went to his cell, spent the night in prayer and reading his Prayer Book. He was up and dressed at 4 a.m., and ate a hearty breakfast.

The police handcuffed him, and walked him from Chester Castle to Glover's Stone, which was the city boundary mark. The police surrounded Murray, as there were great

King Street, Chester. Not much has changed since Victorian days.

The top of Castle Street, which leads from the side of the Crown Court to Lower Bridge Street. Halfway down is the site of the Glover's Stone, which marked the boundary between city and county. All condemned prisoners stopped at the Glover's Stone to be formally handed over from one jurisdiction to the other.

Northgate in Chester. This former gate in the walls of the city was where criminals were hung in public.

crowds waiting to see the execution. They were armed with cutlasses in case of trouble from the crowd of many thousands. About two thirds of the crowd were women, many well dressed. Murray seemed not to notice them.

At the city boundary, Murray and his gaolers left the jurisdiction of the county, and were received by the city authorities. He and the Revd Carberry were placed in a small, black-railed cart provided by the Chester authorities. Murray was manacled and lifted into the cart, the reverend sitting by the condemned man's side. There was a procession of city and police officials, who accompanied the cart as it went to the execution place.

The procession reached the city gaol at 5 a.m. Murray was unshackled and led to the condemned cell via the chapel, where his open coffin lay. The sight did not affect him. He made his devotions, and the rest of the morning the chapel was occupied by priests carrying out the Catholic ceremonial for his soul.

The public were allowed to enter the gaol and see Murray in the condemned cell, which was occasionally crowded with anxious spectators. Murray prayed throughout, none of the proceedings interrupting his devotions.

At 11.30 a.m. the Sheriff entered the cell and cleared it of all spectators except the prison chaplain, Revd Carberry, and various gaol officials. One was a Mr Eaton, who asked Murray if he had any final words. 'I have no declaration to make,' he said. Murray was then led outside to the drop. He ascended the scaffold with a firm step and, after the administration of the sacrament of extreme unction, the hangman carried out his task. It was 12.25 p.m. He died with scarcely a struggle. Murray's smart clothes would become the property of the hangman, who by tradition could claim his client's apparel.

Chapter Seven

The Nantwich Riots, 1841

Democracy is a good thing and hot summer days are pleasant, but Special High Constable Charles Laxton of Nantwich must have been disillusioned by both. Born in Lincolnshire in 1815, he had joined the Metropolitan Police as a young man. Men from the London force had been sent to Birmingham during the 'Bull Ring Riots' of 1838. Charles Laxton was one of these officers, and he had been badly hurt by the crowd. His police experience, and his injuries, may have been the reason why he was chosen to go north in early 1841, to be the Special High Constable at Nantwich. Laxton probably thought he was destined for a quiet life. However, he was in for a hot summer in every sense, facing down very violent election riots, the largest of which was eventually dispersed by heavy rain.

The election of 1841 was fought nationally on issues such as the corn tariffs. In south Cheshire, the dominating political fact was the control of the Grosvenor family and their allies. The Grosvenors were Whigs. There were two election days, Tuesday, 13 July and a Thursday in August.

In south Cheshire, Mr Wilbraham was the Grosvenor candidate. Mr Tollemache, of another ancient and rich Cheshire family, stood for the Tories.

The general opinion was that the Whigs would be returned to power. There was a Tory landslide.

Feelings ran high on all sides, but especially amongst the losing side. There were Election Day riots in Chester, Congleton and Nantwich at the Tuesday poll. In Chester, the Tories were besieged in their headquarters at the Albion Hotel, one activist being saved from a mob by the police. In Congleton, some 300 people chanted and shouted through the streets. In Nantwich, *The Times*' initial report stated that the Riot Act had been read, and troops called in, but that 'nothing serious had occurred'. That was an understatement – there had been a serious riot.

The riotous behaviour began early on the Tuesday polling day in Nantwich, with disturbances in the centre of the town. A mob paraded through the streets with bludgeons, continuing even after the military had been called in. The rioting went on until early the next morning, about 2 or 3 a.m. Charles Laxton had his work cut out that day. He also cut down an effigy of Mr Tollemache that was being waved in front of a magistrate's horse by the rioters, which was later burnt as a mark of contempt. The police at that time were armed with cutlasses, and often used them. That was not the most serious event of that Tuesday.

Tragedy happened when a little convoy of Tollemache supporters left the town by taking two coaches and a 'break' along Welch (now Welsh) Row. Those in the first coach began chanting 'Tollemache for ever'. The coaches were heading in the Chester direction, over the Weaver Bridge, and approaching the Wilbraham Arms, when they were hit by a hail of stones and brickbats.

Brickbats were exactly that – pieces of stone or brick about the shape and size of the flying mammal. Being sharp and heavy they could cut a man's head open. Which they did that day.

A stone-thrower was hiding in a small pathway called Gas Alley. It led to the gasworks, hence the unglamorous name.

Mary Dodd saw Byrne the stone-thrower pick up the stones and hurl them at the coachman, cutting his face. She knew him, and screamed at him, 'God damn you, what are doing – are you going to kill all of the folks on the coach?' As it was, one coach passenger, a tenant of Mr Tollemache, died from his injuries. Several others were also cut and scratched. The coachman himself was covered in wounds and blood, cut by the sharp missiles.

The police arrested the stone-thrower, Mr Byrne, who was tried at Chester Assizes on 6 August for assault and rioting. There were three main witnesses against him, Mary Dodd and her two sisters. Other witnesses testified for him. He was found guilty of assault only, and sentenced to twelve months imprisonment. The judge at Chester said harsh words to Byrne regarding his attitude. Some magistrates muttered about trying his witnesses for perjury.

The Dodd sisters returned to their Nantwich home on the afternoon of Saturday, 7 August. They had a most unpleasant welcome. Large crowds had collected outside their house, which was on Welch Row, and made threats against them. Actual violence happened, so that afternoon the police were called in. They arrested two of the most active rioters. But the police were overwhelmed by the crowd, who released the two men. A rioter was later arrested and held. He appeared in the police court on the next Monday, where he was bailed to appear on Friday 13th. The atmosphere in town was tense and ugly. Any potential witness against the rioters was warned off going to court by 'the mob'.

On Tuesday 9 August the day opened to an eerie silence, as almost all shops were shut. Large mobs congregated in various parts of the town, but especially in Welch Row. Then, as if lit by a spark, the mob exploded into activity, going along Welch Row where they attacked the Dodd sisters' home, smashing windows, then taking out and beating the Dodds with great cruelty. The surprising detail about this attack was that it was carried out by a female mob. The men surrounded the women rioters, protecting them from the police, whilst egging them to more and more violence. Four women were arrested, and promptly taken to the magistrates, where they were sentenced to prison to await trail. As the police were taking one of the women into

Welsh Row, looking from near the aqueduct into town.

Welsh Row nowadays, looking up from the town. The Tollemache party were in a coach going up the road towards the Wilbraham Arms when they were attacked with stones.

The Wilbraham Arms on Welsh Row. Gas Alley, now blocked off, was almost opposite the frontage of this establishment.

The little brick house between the black-and-white building and the Beauty Studio was Superintendent Laxton's home in later years.

custody they were attacked by the mob, so police and prisoner had to flee to safety in the magistrates' office. However, the police managed to catch one of these rioters. He was taken in front of the magistrates, who declared that he should be held in custody pending trial on a charge of riot, assaulting the police and attempting rescue. On taking him to the lock-up, the police were subject to the most ferocious attack of the day. Stones and brickbats were thrown at them. Very large stones, and very sharp brickbats, capable of killing someone if they hit a vital part.

Charles Laxton was injured himself. A large brickbat hit the back of his head, cutting through his hat. Fortunately, the hat was made of tough cloth, so his head was saved. *The Times* reporter stated that the hat was cut as if by a knife. He also wrote that Mr Laxton bore numerous deep bite marks on his hands. These were inflicted by rioters trying to break his grip upon the prisoner in his hands.

Another constable, PC McKinty, was hit on the head by a large stone. He was seriously injured and taken to a surgeon. A third constable was injured in the leg. The mob roamed the town, seeking Tories. The war cry went up when any known Tory was found, 'A Tory! A Tory!', and then the unfortunate was pelted with anything to hand – rocks, stones, mud or worse.

Another witness against Byrne, a Mr Cooper, also had his house attacked. Mr Low, a solicitor who was clerk to the magistrates, had his office attacked. The office was used by the magistrates as a court of petty sessions, so it was a prime target; the railings were torn down and the shrubbery torn up. Mrs Moulton, a daughter of Mrs Dodds, had a lucky escape. Her house was also attacked by a bloodthirsty crowd. Fortunately, she and her family had sized up the situation and fled the building. Someone broke a window and climbed through it, then set fire to the bed curtains. They flared up, and then down, the fire causing little damage. As most of the town houses were made of wood and plaster, the arsonist could have burnt down the whole of Nantwich if Mrs Moulton's home had gone up in flames.

The building on the corner stands on the site of John Dunning's house. He was a neighbour of Superintendent Laxton.

This riot finally ended in the evening when a torrential downpour literally dampened spirits. That must have been a great relief to Mr Laxton and his men. But, the town remained tense. There were no more reports of riotous activity later in the week. Indeed, after that outburst of rage, the town settled back into a period of political apathy. Though local Chester papers and *The Times* of London mentioned these events, the Manchester and north Cheshire papers totally ignored them, even the *Stockport Advertiser*, which was keen to denounce Whig wrongdoings in the election.

John Dunning, the newsagent and former trade unionist, had helped to set up a branch of the Chartists. These were a group of radicals who wanted a 'one man one vote democracy' in 1838. They had no known connection with the 1841 election riots. Their democratic views were not liked by respectable opinion. They were kept under close police supervision. But, as Dunning later wrote, 'Mr Laxton knew us all to be peaceable citizens, he allowed us to read speeches from the *Star* [the Chartist newspaper] sing and talk as we pleased.'

Charles Laxton was not only head of the local police, but also of the fire service. Initially, the two emergency services were one, nationwide. So, after a distinguished police career, Mr Laxton's career went sideways, and he became the town fire chief. On his death in 1882, he was given a fireman's funeral. The cortège was led by the local silver band, whose maestro was his friend, John Dunning.

Chapter Eight

⇒◆⇐

Mary Gallop of Crewe, 1845

The autumn of 1844 was cold, but the activities of one young woman made respectable spines shiver even more than the weather. Her name was Mary Gallop, and she was accused of killing her own father, who had stood between her and her young man. So she decided to remove this obstacle to her happiness. With chilling amorality, she did so with arsenic.

She was an unlikely criminal, born into a poor but honest working family: pious Christians who spent some precious pennies on giving Mary a Sunday school eduction.

Mary was to be 21 years of age on 24 March 1845. She was born in Warrington, to Richard and Mary Gallop. Both were Wesleyan Methodists at first. He remained so, but Mrs Gallop's religious life lapsed somewhat. Mr Gallop earned a small living as a joiner.

Mary went to school – she remembered her father taking her to a Warrington Sunday school when she could barely walk. Later, she went to day school, until she was about 9 years old. However, as her father could not find work, the family moved to Runcorn. That town was experiencing a boom in its chemical and soap industry at the time. Again, her father made sure that she went to school and received some education.

However, his wages were low, so the family moved again, to the Rose Hill district of Liverpool. Again, she was sent to Sunday school, at the Brunswick chapel, and later they moved to Mansfield Street, she going into full-time schooling in Springfield Street. Mr Gallop obtained a better paid post on the railroad, so the family moved again, to Windsor, where they lived for some seven to eight years.

At that time, Mary became a teacher at Pleasant Street Wesleyan Sunday school, and a regular attendee at chapel. The family then included her half sister, one Margaret Smetham. Mary told how she used to assist her with the mangle during the week. Apparently, a comfortable, respectable family living one step up from poverty. But, the seeds of tragedy had been sown.

It began when they were living at Mansfield Street. Mary got to know a neighbour, a man somewhat younger than her. The attraction was apparently mutual, because

Chapel Street, Crewe. Mary Gallop was a Sunday school teacher in the Wesleyan chapel (now demolished) from which the street took its name.

Mill Street, Crewe, showing some of the much modified original houses.

Mill Street, Crewe. The traffic lights stand on a bridge over the River Waldron, usually called the Valley Brook, on which the original mill stood. The railway bridge is modern, and carries the Chester line, which opened in 1840.

when she moved to Windsor (the Liverpool district, not the Thames-side town) he used to visit her and the family. But both of her parents were set against the relationship. The young man was but an apprentice, still not out of his time, when Mary was arrested.

The family moved to the new railway town of Crewe, where Mr Gallop held a job as a carpenter and joiner. A few months after the move, Mary and her mother went back to Liverpool for a few days, and Mary met the young man again. In fact she met him several times, after which they began a correspondence. Mary showed some of the letters to her mother, but never to her father, who was still against the relationship.

About ten months after moving to Crewe, Mary's mother committed suicide. After the funeral, Mary went with her half sister to stay in Liverpool. She kept up her relationship with her young man (whom she did not name). Mary stayed in Liverpool until June, when she returned to Crewe. In July the family expanded. To improve their income, Mr Gallop took in a lodger, one William Frazer, a coach maker.

As the summer went on, Mary pined for her man. And pined some more. By late October, three weeks before his death, she began asking her father for permission to go to Liverpool over Christmas. He refused – in fact he became very angry, and told her in no uncertain terms that he would never give his consent to her having anything to do with the young Liverpolitan. A few days later there was another bitter argument, this time over her cooking skills – or lack of. Mr Gallop accused her of baking potatoes until they were so hard as to be inedible. He threatened to take his belt to her. Mary complained to Margaret that she had had no peace since her mother died. Margaret agreed that her half sister was badly treated by her father. It was not a happy household.

So Mary thought about obtaining a position as a servant in the city. She later opined that that would have made her very happy and avoided all the trouble that happened later.

Her half sister unwittingly put murderous ideas in Mary's mind when she talked about a woman who had poisoned her husband with arsenic, bought under the pretence of rat poison. Now, thought Mary, if she could do that to her father, she would be free to do anything she wanted. She was sure she would not be detected, as her father had suffered from a bowel complaint for several weeks. He was also a local healer – what would nowadays be called a 'first aider'. He plastered wounds and bruises on his injured workmates. So there was little suspicion about his daughter ordering a quantity of strange drugs.

So, she went to the druggist's and purchased a pennyworth of arsenic. Then she had a change of heart – it might not be enough. So she purchased another pennyworth from Mr Abraham the druggist. She put the arsenic into her father's cake. She baked three cakes – one for herself and her half sister, one for the lodger, and the third one for her father, which contained the arsenic. 'If any arsenic got into the flour for the others, it was by accident,' she said.

The cakes were for tea on a Friday night in autumn. However, the plan went awry. She, her half sister and the lodger fell ill after eating their cakes. Mr Gallop did not feel like eating anything solid, and so his cake was put away in a cupboard.

From about midnight the others were all vomiting, and had stomach pains. Mary was extremely ill. When she awoke the next morning, she was so ill or nervous that she fainted. Mr Gallop was well enough to take some food, bread and milk for breakfast then some slices of beef in the afternoon.

Margaret ate some more of the cake on that Saturday, and fell ill again. She spent the rest of the weekend in bed.

Mary did not. She gathered up her strength and went again to the druggist for some more arsenic. Later that afternoon, at about 3 p.m., the poison was mixed with some arrowroot. The mixture was left for her father. He was expected home from work at 4 p.m. For the past three weeks, ever since his stomach pains began, he had soothed them by taking a mixture of arrowroot, milk and sugar. Mary left the arrowroot powder, with its addition, for her father, who put some milk into it to make a soothing drink. He was taken ill soon afterwards, and died the next morning.

That Saturday evening Mary told Margaret not to eat any more cake. That same evening, 2 November, Mr Gallop became very ill. He told the others that he was very sick. He told Frazer that he had been ill ever since taking the arrowroot. The lodger tried a portion of the arrowroot mixture – it was still in its bowl, covered with a strange yellow froth. Frazer tried a taste – he found it hot, 'like cayenne pepper'. Meanwhile Mr Gallop was being sick. He vomited at intervals all that night. Frazer said that a doctor must be called for, and went himself to Mr Stevenson. He saw him three times that night, and gave Mr Gallop some mixture. Frazer asked about the bowl of arrowroot – it had been taken away by Mary, and thoroughly washed.

Mary remained by her father's bedside until 1 a.m. She got up at 6 a.m.

Waking up on the Sunday morning, Mr Gallop drank some tea brought to him by Mary. Some of Mr Gallop's vomit had been collected in a large mug and put under the bed. At about half past seven that Sunday morning, Mr Gallop died.

Mary was shocked by the death – on that point everyone was agreed. Roughly an hour and a half from the death, she asked Frazer to get her a free rail pass for Liverpool. She claimed that she wanted to see her sister. He declined to let her do so.

Mr Gallop's body was laid out by a woman named Miller. At 11 a.m. that morning, an assistant constable, Michael Kenty, came to call. He had heard about the death and all sudden deaths had to be investigated. He questioned Mary. She said her father had taken the arrowroot at 4 p.m., but later, around 7 p.m., he had complained that the arrowroot had had a bad taste about it. He told Mary to go to the shop and ask about. She went to Mrs Pickersgill's shop. That good lady insisted that her products were pure, and that she only sold good arrowroot. Mary also told the constable that her father had been worried by rats and mice in the house, and had sent her to the druggist to get *nux vomica* (a natural source of strychnine used as a stomach medicine). Mary also said that her sister was aware of the rats, and had seen one last Thursday.

The policeman's suspicions were aroused. He asked Mary to take what she wanted from the drawers. She chose a handkerchief, which Kenty took from her, and found a small paper packet in her hand. Written on it were the words 'nux vomica. Poison'. Mary explained that she had purchased the poison about a fortnight before, from Mr Abraham for one penny. It was to kill rats. By this time more officers had arrived. Assistant Constable Kenty searched the house with the help of Constables Boydell and Nash, and in the presence of Mary, Margaret and Frazer the lodger. Kenty found items of food in the cupboard, which he gave to PC Boydell. Mary went to a chest of drawers, and was seen to cover a blue paper with some clothes. Kenty took the paper and accused her of putting it in the drawer. She denied all knowledge, and said Kenty must have put it there. It was 'salter' and found to contain arrowroot. Kenty took her into custody. He also searched her pockets and found another bit of paper, again with writing on it. This was 'two pennyworth of anser [sic]'. Some 200 grains of arrowroot were taken away for analysis at Liverpool.

Mary was taken into custody and an inquest was ordered. The coroner's court opened the following Tuesday, 5 November. The Knutsford coroner, Mr Roscoe, was in charge of proceedings. He heard some of the evidence above, and a statement from the doctor who had examined Mr Gallop's body. He said that Mr Gallop's mouth showed evidence of ingesting a corrosive substance – such as arsenic.

The coroner's jury quickly came to a conclusion – a charge of 'Wilful Murder against Mary Gallop'. She was remanded in custody at Chester Castle to await her trial at the Winter Assizes. Her trial opened on Friday, 6 December 1844. News of her crime had spread around the country. The Assize at Chester Castle was packed with curious spectators. Many people noticed an odd fact. Though everyone looked at her, she looked at nobody. In fact, she seemed to be indifferent to what was going on around her. She just looked blankly around the courtroom. This strange behaviour supported the popular opinion that she was mad.

The evidence given was damning. Mr William Abraham, the druggist of Crewe, confirmed that the prisoner had come to him to buy 'crowfeet'. That was the local name for *nux vomica*. She had it about a week before Mr Gallop's death. She said it was to poison mice. She also had aniseed meal. This seemingly innocuous substance was used to flavour arsenic, and make it attractive to mice and rats. Mr Gallop had prescribed it to other people.

She had later brought a piece of paper to Mr Abraham, on which was written the order 'One pennyworth of arsenic for destroying rats'. Mary had claimed there were rats in the kitchen. Mr Abraham told her that arsenic was a very strong poison, and gave details of its effects. Promising to be careful, Mary left with the arsenic wrapped in a white paper with 'Poison – handle with care' written upon it.

Two or three weeks later, she had come again to Mr Abraham with an order for more arsenic. This was provided. She said that the house still suffered from rats. She was told to throw away any unused arsenic. Mr Abraham told the court that he had never sold any *nux vomica* to her. Though the label 'nux vomica – poison' found on her by Kenty was in his handwriting, he had not sold any to her, despite his earlier statement to the contrary.

Further evidence was provided by Dr George Stevenson, a surgeon of Crewe. He told the court he had tested the arrowroot specimen given him by the police. It

The Bridge of Sighs over the canal in Chester. This bridge linked the old prison with the former court. Many miscreants passed over this bridge on their way to prison.

contained arsenic. Upon examining the body, he found burns such as would be caused by arsenic or some other corrosive substance.

Mr Stevenson sent Mr Gallop's stomach and stomach contents to David Waldie, chemist of Liverpool. He found a small quantity of arsenic. Mr Kenty had sent to him 200 grains of arrowroot. Mr Waldie found the sample to be composed of equal quantities of arrowroot and arsenic.

Mary's defence lawyer, Mr Trafford, took an unusual line of defence. He raised the possibility that Mr Gallop might have been treating himself with arsenic. Gallop was an amateur physician, with an extensive knowledge of medicines and their properties. Having suffered from a bowel complaint, he might have decided to treat himself.

Mr Trafford pointed out that only a small amount of arsenic had been found in the dead man's stomach. Not enough to prove that Mary had deliberately tried to poison her father.

His third line of defence was to refer to Mary's mother. She had been suffering from insanity when pregnant with Mary, and had committed suicide. The defence counsel said that as insanity was inherited, then Mary was surely mad.

The judge summed up the case in great detail. He concluded that the evidence was purely circumstantial, but this was the case in 99 out of 100 poisoning cases. The jury did not retire to consider a verdict. They discussed amongst themselves for a short time, and then pronounced a verdict of guilty.

The judge said that Mary had been found guilty, on evidence that could leave no doubt, of the murder of her own father, and that murder was committed by the most odious and detestable of all means – that of poison. He could see no signs of remorse or repentance from Mary, so it was impossible for him to show *her* any mercy. She was sentenced to be hanged.

The sentence was due to be carried out just after Christmas, on Saturday, 28 December 1844.

Many in Chester had sent petitions to the judges for mercy. Respectable opinion thought that such petitions were a good reason to ignore pleas of mercy, and defy public opinion by employing the full rigour of the law, to show the mob who was boss.

Nonetheless, there were grounds for mercy. On strictly legal procedures, the judge had not told the jury that if they had any doubt they must acquit the prisoner. There were doubts as to her sanity. Also, the 'confession' which she was later said to have produced, was no such thing. A Dissenting Minister, Mr C. Rowe, had asked her various questions, to which she replied with a single 'Yes' or 'No'.

All doubts on the matter were ended when a telegram arrived at Chester Castle from the then Home Secretary, Sir J. Graham, which stated that he had found no grounds for mercy. The prison staff gave Mary no false hopes. She was immediately informed of the Home Secretary's decision, and apparently went into shock, but soon recovered to her former unnatural calmness.

She was moved from the castle to Chester city gaol. The gallows were being made ready. The crowd was gathering to watch Mary's removal from one prison to the other. So the authorities decided to prevent any trouble by moving her at midnight. The local police superintendent, Mr Hill, came to the castle with the appropriate documents soon after midnight. Mary appeared, supported on the arms of the matron of the castle, Mrs Bennion. This lady put a thick veil over Mary's head and shoulders, and let the police gently pick her up into a small cart. She went into it 'with the ease and composure of one going on a pleasure excursion' reported *The Times*.

The Dissenting Minister, Mr Rowe, took his seat at her left hand. This was by her special request. On the right sat police sergeant Doherty. Walking alongside the small cart were a number of policemen. Behind the chaise were Superintendent Hill and Mr Haswell, governor of the city gaol. The mournful procession made its way through the dark, cold late-night city streets.

On coming to the city gaol, a shaft of moonlight lit up the gallows. Mary's composure left her and she nearly fainted. When the cart stopped Mr Hill had to lift her out of it, as she was utterly helpless. Mr Hill carried her in his arms, upstairs to a room in jail where she was cared for by the jail matron and Mrs Heswall. Mary had less than twelve hours to live.

At half past eleven that morning, accompanied by two female warders, she went to the prison chapel for a final service. The enormity of what had happened – what would shortly happen – seemed to finally hit her. She was allowed a brief time alone in her room for prayer.

Sign explaining the history of the bridge and prison. The old prison had a dungeon whose only air inlet was a small pipe. One gang of sheep rustlers silenced an imprisoned comrade by stuffing the air pipe with wool, thus suffocating him.

The executioner then entered the prison room and bound her arms. Incapable of standing up, she was carried in a chair to the gallows. At the foot of the gallows, the reverend gentlemen, prison chaplain Mr Eaton and Mr Rowe, said their final farewells. The executioner asked for and got her pardon. He shook her hand in a final gesture, then pulled the bolt.

As she was still sitting on the chair, the drop was too short. Instead of dying instantly, Mary was slowly strangled. There was an awful silence when she finally died.

That was not quite the end of the affair. A few weeks later, in January 1845, the Bishop of Chester and other worthies wrote a letter to *The Times* clarifying some issues. They had signed the petition for mercy for Mary. However, some had said that in doing so they had thereby showed sympathy for parricide (nowadays referred to as patricide). They refuted such talk, and said they had no sympathy or mercy for such a crime, but had thought that there were grounds for mercy in Mary's case.

Chapter Nine

⟫◆⟪

'I Will Die Hardly':
The Adlington Murder, 1847

It is often thought that mugging is a modern crime, though in fact the word and deed were known in Victorian times. The word 'mug' is criminal slang for street robbery with actual or threatened violence. However, not every potential target for a 'mug' was an easy victim, as two criminals found to their cost in 1847.

They intended to rob anyone walking along a particular road, anyone at all. They had no single individual in mind. Unfortunately for them, the individual walking along the road at that time was Mr James Ernill. Contemporary newspaper reports describe him as a corn merchant, though trade directories list him as a grocer in Macclesfield. Victorian businessmen usually had interests in various enterprises, to spread the risks in an insecure economy. He probably came from Mellor in north Derbyshire, and was in early middle age, a hale and hearty man when the incident occurred.

It happened at about 3 p.m. on the afternoon of 11 February 1847, as he was walking home to Macclesfield. His route took him through a wooded road at Adlington, near Prestbury. Prestbury is now one of the richest commuter villages in the UK, but then it was a mining village, and the area was rather lonely and remote. However, there was a road and a canal nearby. By the main road was a wood, and Mr Ernill saw two men come out of the Wych Wood, and walk behind him at a steady pace, keeping about a quarter of mile away from him. All seemed normal until one of the men came forward. He was later identified as William Bates, a 30-year-old Irishman and illiterate joiner. Bates was dark in complexion, with a 'very contracted and low brow'. He was also of a passionate temper, quick to anger and always keen to take offence.

He came up to his victim, and then seized Mr Ernill around the breast, held a pistol at the merchant's head, uttered 'vile oaths', and threatened 'Your watch and your purse this minute, or you're a dead man.' His partner in crime added force to the threat by pointing his pistol at Mr Ernill's left ear and repeating the threat. The accomplice was a younger and fairer man, also Irish, with at least two names, his real one and an alias. Both were surprised by Mr Ernill's reaction. Mr Ernill stayed silent for about a minute, looking both men up and down, before saying that if they wanted his property they would find him a tougher customer than they expected.

The younger robber, Walmsley, alias Mawdsley, took this reply badly. He knocked Mr Ernill down and a fight began, both men going down several times. Mr Ernill kept fighting until he was knocked down again. He shouted at his attackers, 'I shall die but once, and you may depend upon it that I will die hardly.'

The fight continued for a few minutes until the arrival of an old man called John Hardman, who had been working at a canal bridge a short distance away. He had seen what was going on, and so rushed to help Mr Ernill. At the sight of Mr Hardman, and his shovel, the two robbers fled.

Being helped to his feet by Mr Hardman, Mr Ernill found himself bereft of his watch chain, two seals, and two keys. Mr Ernill's shoulder blade was also broken; he had indeed fought hardly. The redoubtable Mr Hardman ensured that Mr Ernill was well, called for help, and then ran after the robbers.

The commotion had aroused the neighbourhood. There were many people working in the area, either on the farms or the canal. Working in a barn at Royle's Bridge, on the canal bank, was a Mr Thomas Wyatt. He heard the noise, and went to find its source. He joined a small crowd of bargees and labourers.

This group formed a posse that went after the robbers. The robbers went along the canal bank, then across some fields into Blake Hey Wood pursued by the crowd. The pursuit was eventful. Every so often, the two pursued would turn and point their pistols at the crowd, threatening to shoot anyone who came to close. Each man had two pistols, and each man threatened to blow the brains out of any witness.

One of the crowd, a Mr William Wyatt, brother of Thomas, told the men to put down their pistols and deliver themselves to the law for a fair trial. They had attempted to rob a gentleman on the highway: if innocent they would be set free, but if guilty they must be prosecuted.

This earnest appeal did not have the desired effect. Instead of giving themselves up, the two villains became more determined to escape. In fact, soon after the plea, Bates took off his hat, put it down beside him, and said, 'I swear by this book, by St Patrick, and the virtue of Jesus, Oyez once! Oyez twice! And here goes the last time – so help me God if you come any further I'll shoot the first man!' He waved his gun around to emphasise his threat.

With that dramatic cry, the two felons then ran into Blake Hey Wood, followed by a crowd of about twenty people. William Wyatt was in the lead. As he was about to seize Bates, the prey turned around and fired the pistol he had in his left hand.

The ball entered Mr Wyatt's body a little below the breastbone, almost coming out of his back, though it settled between the muscle and skin. Mr William Wyatt's brother, Thomas, was at that time getting his hands on Mawdsley, who also fired his gun. That pistol ball went through the fleshy part of Thomas's arm, causing no serious injury. The crowd soon captured both Mawdsley and Bates. On their persons was found evidence of their crime – Mr Ernill's watch, chain, seals and keys.

The injured William Wyatt was carried home, where he died from his injuries the next day.

The two robbers were delivered to the police constable at Poynton. No reports exist of what state they were in, but having just shot down an unarmed and innocent local, the crowd were unlikely to have treated the miscreants with care.

Mawdsley's coat was taken off him by the constable, James Bowers. In its pockets were found eight percussion caps for firing the guns. Bates was taken to the Macclesfield magistrate. Both were remanded until a full trial at Chester Assizes.

The case aroused great interest and excitement in the county. Everyone eagerly awaited the trial, which took place on Saturday, 8 April 1848, at Chester.

Despite the lapse of more than a year, public interest in the trial had not waned – in fact it had grown so much that the press described the courtroom as 'filled to suffocation'.

The judge was Mr Justice Williams. For the defence was Mr Temple, the prosecutor being Messrs Egerton and Brandt. Reports said that Bates was unfeeling about the affair. In fact, he did not seem to worry about the threat of hanging – he was more concerned about going blind, as he had a cataract in his eye. Mawdsley's face appeared strained and he appeared to have been weeping.

Mr Ernill had already given his testimony when a surprising development happened. Despite being illiterate, Bates declared that he wanted to dismiss his defence counsel, Mr Temple, and conduct his own defence. If the court would allow him to do so, he would cross-examine the witnesses himself, and so would be able to prove his innocence. Quivering with emotion, he demanded justice.

Judge Williams asked Mawdsley if he wanted to defend himself.

'I would rather leave it to the gentleman who has it in hand for me,' he replied. It was a wise decision. When asked by the judge, Bates confirmed that he wished to defend himself. 'If I get justice,' he replied.

The judge asked if he wanted any witnesses recalled.

'Yes, all of them,' he replied, to the judge's surprise.

Bates then confirmed the old lawyers' adage that a man who defends himself has a fool as a client.

As all the witnesses returned, they were harangued by Bates 'at great length and in a very violent manner'. Bates complained that the judge was not writing down all the witness statements.

'My questions are as important as those asked by the counsel,' he exploded.

He then appealed to the press and public to back up his case. He finished after cross-examining police constable Bowers and two medical men.

Mr Temple, the defence counsel, then took up the metaphorical cudgels on Mawdsley's behalf. In a long and impassioned argument, he set out the case for the prisoners. He argued that they had a justified fear of being attacked by the mob following them. If the jury believed that they fired in genuine fear, then they could claim to be acting in self-defence, and the murder charge could be reduced to manslaughter. If the guns had been fired accidentally, then there was no case to answer. Indeed, if they had intended murder, they would have fired the guns before.

Mr Temple maintained there was no intent to murder, the guns being used only for intimidation.

Bates was allowed to sum up his defence case. In a long rambling tale, he told the jury that the fatal shot had been fired by Mawdsley, not him. Bates maintained that he had not fired until attacked by bludgeons wielded by persons in the crowd.

He also told the court that he and Mawdsley had been without food for that day and the previous one. Instead of tackling Mr Ernill, they had merely asked him for relief. If he had just given them 6d or a shilling, then all this trouble would have been avoided.

Mr Justice Williams summed up all the evidence. He told the jury that there must be substantial doubt to justify a not guilty verdict. If they had no doubt as to guilt, then, despite their personal feelings, they must bring in a verdict of guilty.

The jury then retired to discuss their verdict. About half an hour later, they returned to announce a verdict of guilty.

Bates nearly collapsed from shock, but soon recovered his former tough guy persona. Mawdsley asked to make a statement, not a long one, just the one remark: 'Poverty was the occasion of it. Had I been paid my honest hard earnings, I should not have been there.'

The judge earnestly exhorted the men to use their last days on earth to seek the mercy of God. He then donned the black cap and pronounced the sentence of death in the proscribed manner. Their bodies would be buried inside the prison precincts.

Bates said he would die very cheerfully. They were then both led away. Four witnesses were recommended for rewards by Mr Townsend, who stated that Mr Hardman should be rewarded, but he would consider the matter.

In prison, both prisoners were reported to be attending to religion with great zeal. Appeals for clemency were made. For Mawdsley, there was a respite: he was ordered to be detained at Her Majesty's Pleasure. Mawdsley was said to be extremely grateful for the reprieve. However, he also tried to get a reprieve for Bates. Now, Bates had claimed in court that Mawdsley had fired the fatal shot, despite around a dozen witnesses to the contrary. That attempt to shift both the blame and the death sentence had failed. But Mawdsley now claimed that he had indeed fired the fatal shot, so he was equally as guilty as Bates. So, if he was reprieved, then surely natural justice would allow Bates to be respited also. His argument failed. No reprieve came for Bates.

The two men also confessed to being professional criminals. They had claimed to be poor working men, though poor men would surely have pawned their guns and ammunition for food, rather than taking up armed robbery. In particular, they admitted to an earlier highway robbery committed in Manchester. Two fellow Irishmen named O'Brien and Connelly had been tried and condemned for that crime and were serving a fifteen-year sentence in Kirkgate Gaol. Upon receipt of Bates's and Mawdsley's confessions, they were released.

Bates was executed in public at Chester, at the west entrance of the city gaol, on 22 April 1848. His death was watched by the usual large crowd.

Chapter Ten

Chester Child Murders, 1856

William Jackson was an upholsterer by trade. He was of above average height, at 5ft 10ins, with a dark complexion and a sullen face. In 1856 he was 35 years old, and regarded as well educated. Though he had a trade, he did not practice it frequently and was reported to have been living a very irregular life, despite having a wife and four children to feed and clothe. Not surprisingly, his wife grew tired of his dissolute ways and left him, going to Manchester with two of the four children. The other two, John, aged 6, and his 7-year-old sister Mary Jane, were put under the care of one of Jackson's two sisters, Mrs Betsy Hancock, who lived with her husband Charles at Foundry Street in Chester. She became unable to care for the children in late September 1856 and, on the 27th of that month, she sent them to live at a friend's house in nearby Handbridge. She sent the children with her servant girl, 14-year-old Mary Anne Evans. That September morning, Mary walked through the pouring rain to Handbridge. Despite the rain, both children were barefoot. She went to the Coach & Horses public house, the landlady of which, Mrs Rogers, was a friend of the Jackson family. Mrs Hancock hoped that the Rogers could put the children up in their pub. Mr Jackson was at the pub that morning. She met him at as he was standing at the front door of the pub. She said to him, 'If you please, Mrs Hancock has sent the two children.'

'What did you bring them here for?'

'Mrs Hancock has sent them,' she said again.

'You must take them back again.'

She explained that Mrs Hancock would not take them back. Mary then went back out into the rain.

She left the children with their father, and went away. As she left, she saw the children enter Mrs Roger's house and sit down. Mrs Rogers said to Jackson that she could not keep the children. Jackson said, 'I don't want you to keep the children.' He then went to the door and called out to Mary. In the rain she did not hear him and kept on walking. William Jackson took the children out. To all later enquiries by Mrs

Handbridge in the snow. Handbridge was a separate town from Chester, just south of the old city.

Another view of nineteenth-century buildings in Handbridge.

Rogers, he just muttered that they were safe and well at a friend's house. She made many enquiries, as Jackson stayed at the pub.

All seemed well for a week or two, but as time went on and nothing was heard from or about the children, suspicions grew. Rumours flew around the city that William had killed the children. On Monday 20 October, Mrs Rogers mentioned these rumours to Jackson. He replied that Chester was full of malicious gossips.

Some of the neighbours contacted Mrs Jackson in Manchester. She came back to Chester on Tuesday 21 October and went straight to the city's Chief Constable, Mr Hill, telling him she feared something dreadful had happened to her children. The interview with Mrs Jackson occurred too late in the evening for anything immediate to be done. However, the following morning the Chief Constable went directly to the city magistrates for an order to arrest Mr Jackson on suspicion of murder. By then the city was rife with rumours about the missing children.

Mr James Broadway, a dentist, met Jackson early that day and noticed that he was very low. They met a man named Jones, who went off with Jackson. A little later, Mr Broadway met Mrs Rogers at the Coach & Horses. She was crying. When asked why, she replied that Mrs Jackson was here, and it is said that her husband had made away with his children. 'I've just seen him,' said Mr Broadway, who then ran out and saw him again. Mr Broadway said, 'Bill, here is a fine thing against you. Your wife is in town.'

'Well,' he replied, 'she can go back the same way she came.' Mr Broadway got straight to the point. 'They say you have made away with your two children.'

He replied, 'So I have, from her and my sister. She could not have had much love for them, or she would not have turned them out on the day she did.'

'That may be,' said Mr Broadway, 'but I think your wife ought to be satisfied as to where they are.'

Jackson replied, 'I know where they are; they are in those hands that will take good care of them.' The two men then parted company.

Mr Hill put one of his best men on Jackson's trail. Sergeant Charles Speed soon found Jackson at the city walls, near Nun's Gardens. He told Jackson that he must ask him some plain questions. He was suspected of having 'destroyed' two of his children, and if he did not account for them then he was to be taken into custody. Jackson replied that 'they are all right, and my wife will never know where they are.' PC Whittaker promptly took him along to the police station. He was questioned again, in the presence of Mr Hill, he repeated that statement about the children. PC Whittaker repeated the same question at a half hour interview; Jackson was asked three times in all, and three times he gave the same reply.

That was an unsatisfactory answer, so later that Wednesday afternoon, Jackson appeared in court, and was ordered to say where the children were by the magistrate. Mrs Jackson had made an affidavit, accusing him of murdering the children. In reply to all questions put to him by the magistrate, Colonel Lloyd simply replied 'they are safe'. This was not thought to be a satisfactory answer, so he was remanded in custody until the next day, when he was to appear before the full bench to give a full account of the children's fate and whereabouts.

Mr Hill started to investigate. His officers soon discovered that on the last day the children were seen alive, on 27 September, Jackson had been seen going from his sister's house with the children, towards a pit hole, at the farthest end of a nursery garden owned by a Mr Rogers. That day, the 27th, had been a very wet one. Jackson had been seen going through torrents of rain with a little bare-headed child in his arms. He went into the garden and was lost sight of. The witness who saw him that day recalled that Jackson had not been seen for some days afterwards. On Thursday 23 October, Mr Hill sent an officer with a dog to dig at the spot.

Police constable Thomas Whittaker set off promptly for the nursery garden.

Man and dog got to the site at 9.45 a.m. The retriever scratched and sniffed and pawed around the garden. Within a few minutes the dog started to scrape at some disturbed soil over a small pit. The soil appeared to have been recently disturbed. The policeman was soon disturbed himself. After picking up a shovel and digging away a few clods of earth, he saw a small naked foot sticking up from the ground. He went straightaway back to the police station to alert Hill and other officers. They all dashed to the site, armed with spades and picks. Some fast and furious digging revealed the corpse of a little boy, lying face downwards, minus cap, shoes and socks. More digging revealed some water. When the pit had been bailed out, another body was recovered. This was a little girl, again face downwards, but with a bonnet and cloak on. The children's corpses were taken from their grave and looked at. The cause of death was obvious. Each had had its throat slit. They appeared to have had their throats cut in such a way as to slash the carotid artery without cutting along the whole throat.

The stiff and distorted little bodies were put on a handcart and taken first to the city workhouse so that the little girl's clothes could be removed and washed for identification purposes. News of the discovery had spread fast around the city. From Handbridge to the workhouse, the road was lined with spectators, mostly women, who wept openly and bitterly for the poor children.

After the clothes were taken off, the bodies were deposited in the dead house (mortuary) at 11.45 a.m.; just two hours after the search had started. At noon, Mr Jackson was scheduled to appear before the Prentice Court for his magisterial hearing. He did not know that the bodies had been discovered. The city, however, did know – there was a large and angry crowd gathering outside the building.

The public gallery was crowded with spectators, and it took a while for order to be restored in court. The magistrates included the Mayor, Dr P. Jones and Colonel Lloyd.

Mr Hill told the court that the prisoner was charged with wilfully murdering two of his children. Two bodies had been found that morning, and he felt convinced that he would be able to charge the prisoner with the crime.

Jackson was reported to have 'firmly clenched his teeth' and seemed to conduct himself with indifference.

Mrs Elizabeth Rogers was the first witness to give evidence. She was a remote relative of Mrs Jackson, and wife of the landlord of the Coach & Horses public house in Handbridge. She had known the children well since their birth. They had been in the habit of coming to her house, and had last done so on 27 September. Jackson himself was there, no doubt moaning about his troubles, and she recalled telling him that she could not keep the children. She said that he had replied, 'I do not want you.' He then went up to Handbridge, returning after half an hour. He took the little girl away. She had a bonnet on, which Mrs Rogers said she would know again. The recovered bonnet was then shown to her. Mrs Rogers collapsed in tears. After recovering her composure, she said that Jackson had returned to her house after about half or three quarters of an hour, and taken away the little boy. Later that day, before teatime, she had asked him where he had taken the children. 'To a friend's house,' he had replied. She had several conversations with him about the children over the next few weeks. He never gave her a direct answer, but always told her that they were safe. She began to suspect that they had been deposited in the workhouse. In fact, she said, she had asked him yesterday morning (22 September) and he had told her they were in Boughton, safe and well at a friend's house.

Jackson was invited to ask Mrs Rogers any questions. He muttered, 'I have nothing to ask her.' Elizabeth Thomas was next. She explained that she was a single woman from Handbridge. She washed and cleaned for Mrs Rogers, and was in the house when Jackson and the children arrived. The little girl explained that their guardian, Jackson's sister, could keep them no longer. Mr Jackson looked very low at that time. Mrs Rogers had cut some bread and butter for the children. Yesterday, she was with Mrs Rogers when she had asked about the children. He had replied that they were safe enough, but that neither their mother nor their aunt would ever see them again. He would not forgive his sister Betsy as long as she lived.

A local tobacconist, Mr Joseph Haynes, stated that during his dinner break on 27 September last, he had seen Jackson coming up Mr Ducker's rope walk with a child in his arms: 'It was raining fast and the child was dripping wet.' Mr Haynes said he knew Jackson, but not the children. He saw Jackson head directly for a hatch leading from the rope walk to Roger's garden, then to the place where the bodies were found. He did not see Jackson again for a few days.

Jackson again declined to ask any questions when invited to do so.

The relevant police officers, John Hill the Chief Constable, and PC Thomas Whittaker, then gave their evidence. The proceedings ended with Jackson being remanded in custody until the following Monday. He had refused to question any of the witnesses.

On Monday 27 October, the case was heard at the Exchange Hall in Chester. It was a large hall, capable of holding between 1,500 and 2,000 people. It was crowded that day and at least as many people were outside the building. Several hundred people tried and failed to enter the building.

The magistrates' bench was full, with the Mayor presiding. The witnesses from the inquest were again called, and repeated their testimonies. A new witness was called. She was Jackson's sister, Mrs Hancock. She had also identified the bodies, and confirmed that the clothes found on the bodies were those worn by the children on the last day they were seen alive.

Another witness, William Green of Mr Ducker's rope walk, said that he had seen Jackson coming from the direction of the pit in which the bodies had been found, on 27 September. Everyone had an excellent memory for that day because of the fierce rainstorm.

The Crown Court at Chester. The castle is on the right, out of view. Castle Street is on the left.

The entrance to the Crown Court at Chester.

Another witness was a friend of Jackson's. He was Francis Cotreave, who had known Jackson for a long time. He gave his version of events of 27 September. He recalled the torrential rain of that day. J. Jackson had called at his house. His boots were very dirty, and from the elbow down to his hand his coat was covered in slush and mud. Having seen the hole in which the children were found, he could confirm that the mud on Jackson was the same colour as the mud in the hole. Jackson had asked for a brush and some water with which to wash himself.

Mr Brittain, the local surgeon, gave evidence of his autopsy. The little girl had an incision three inches long across the left side of the neck. Despite first appearance, this had not cut the carotid artery in any way, but had severed the jugular vein. Her right thumb was separated at the second joint, as though she had tried to fight off her attacker. The little boy had a cut across his neck that had severed both the jugular vein and carotid artery. Both children would have died instantly from their wounds.

Mr Hill finished the proceedings by stating that that was the police case. The bench asked Jackson if he wanted to say anything. 'Nothing at all,' Jackson replied, before being committed to stand trail at the Assizes on a charge of wilful murder.

A coroner's jury sat later that day and also gave a verdict of 'Wilful Murder'.

The trial took place at Chester Crown Court on Friday 5 December, before Mr Baron Alderson. The prosecutors were Messrs Swetenham and Lloyd. Jackson attempted to defend himself, but later on, as the trial proceeded, he changed his mind. He called for a defence counsel, specifically a Mr MacIntyre. He was called to court, and agreed to defend Jackson, though he confined himself to summing up the case to the jury.

Also in the court was a large crowd. Mr Swetenham started the proceedings with a statement of the prosecution case. The prosecution witnesses were called forward, and gave the testimonies that they had given in the earlier preliminary hearings. Mary Anne, the servant girl, confirmed the two children's identities.

She used to dress the children and knew their clothes well. The clothing shown in court was indeed that worn by the children on the last day they were seen alive. She also said that she and Mr Rogers had identified the dead bodies when the corpses were laid out at the workhouse.

Jackson heard Mrs Roger's statement. He did not ask her any questions when invited to do so. He did not make any statements or ask questions of any of the other witnesses. In fact, he produced no evidence or arguments for his case at all. He gave no information as to who was supposed to have cared for the children or where they had been kept. He could produce no witnesses who could prove that the children were alive after 27 September. He could not name anyone who had a motive for killing the children. His defence seemed hopeless.

Mr MacIntyre, Jackson's freshly appointed defence counsel, did the best he could with the brief. He eloquently addressed the jury. He went for an emotional appeal, telling the jury that it was improbable that a father would destroy his own children. The evidence given had been purely circumstantial. But even if the jury convicted on that evidence, they had to admit that such a deed could have been done when the prisoner was suffering under a sudden paroxysm, and if such were the case he should be found guilty of manslaughter, not murder.

Baron Alderson dryly pointed out that if that were the case, it would still be murder, because the child could not be capable of proper provocation. Mr MacIntyre continued, pointing out that a murder conviction must be based upon absolute certainty, and that if the jury had any doubt, they had a duty to give the prisoner the benefit of that doubt.

In summing up, the judge told the jury that they must decide according to the truth, and only the truth. The question was not one 'of murder or manslaughter, but murder or nothing'. To find a verdict of manslaughter would be positively to disregard their oath.

The jury took his words to heart. Without leaving their box, they consulted amongst themselves for a few minutes, then returned a verdict of Guilty. At that, a smile was seen to play on Jackson's face for a moment, after which he resumed his usual indifferent pose. He did pass a piece of paper to the judge, upon which he claimed there was a confession. Judge Alderson looked at it, read it, and threw it away. He said it contained no information and was not signed either, and was therefore invalid.

The Clerk of the Crown asked him to explain why a sentence of death should not be passed upon him. Jackson said nothing at all. He appeared to be unmoved. Baron Alderson then put on his black cap. He gave a moving speech, denouncing the crime and hoping fervently that Jackson would find mercy in the afterlife, if he begged Christ for mercy. The speech affected almost everyone in court. There were no dry eyes amongst the lawyers, the jury or the crowd. There was only one pair of eyes that stayed dry: Jackson remained totally unmoved. After the speech, he leisurely picked up his hat, and casually walked away from the dock.

The execution date was set for Saturday 22 December, a dark, damp day. Long before 6 a.m. large crowds were assembling. Jackson left his cell a 7.45 a.m. for a final church service and was apparently much affected by it. Though his warders were affected, Jackson allowed himself to be trussed and taken to the gallows without any sign of emotion. He stepped firmly upon the drop while the hangman, Calcraft, put a cap over his head and adjusted the rope. Jackson told the chaplain that he died confessing his sins. The chaplain, Revd Mr Kilner, blessed him and shook his hand. The bolt was drawn and William Jackson fell into eternity without a struggle.

Chapter Eleven

A Fatal Night Out, Birkenhead, 1856

Victorian Birkenhead was the fastest growing town in Europe, an industrial centre and port town that was both rough and tough. Sectarian riots were frequent, as were murders.

One particular murder occurred after a pleasant night out. Thomas Smith, a labourer, went for some drinks after work with friends. It was a crisp winter's night just before Christmas in 1856 – 23 December. The ale was good, so Smith had some more. And some more. By early the next morning he was rather drunk, but still thirsty for more. Victorian pubs had flexible opening hours and could stay open all night. But publicans need to sleep sometime, and Mr Softly, the landlord, and his wife were not best pleased when Smith began thumping at their pub door at half past one in the morning, shouting at them to wake up and draw him some ale. Mrs Softly told him in no uncertain terms that she would not let him in and certainly would not draw any ale. So he kicked in the pub's door panel.

Mrs Softly came downstairs followed by Patrick Fox, a groom lodging with the Softlys. They pushed Smith away, then Fox went to find a constable. Police officer William Vaughan soon appeared on the scene. He saw Smith, his companion Breen and the lady publican all standing outside in the cold. The two tiddly men said they just wanted a glass of beer. PC Vaughan told Smith, 'You had better go home young man; you have had enough to drink.' Mrs Softly told PC Vaughan that if Mr Smith paid for the damaged door she would not lay any charges. The drunken man moaned that he had not got any money to pay for the repairs. She then told him to go away, which he and Breen did rather reluctantly, followed by PC Vaughan.

The incident was overheard by a cab driver, Joseph Lawton, who had been drinking in the Softlys' pub. He saw two men go away, then Smith hurrying back again. When about 25 yards from the pub, Lawton saw PC Vaughan lay his hands upon Smith, and was heard to say, 'Go home my good man.' Smith and PC Vaughan then left.

A short time after, a man named Croft ran up the street, shouting to Joseph for help. Together, the two men went to the corner of Bridge Street and Hamilton Square, where they found PC Vaughan staggering along the street, his uniform stained with his own blood. Joseph Lawton put his arms around the policeman to support him, and heard him moan, 'Joe, I'm stabbed, I'm done.'

James Croft, a resident of Bidstone near Birkenhead, told the trial that he recollected being in Bridge Street on the morning in question with a shandry – a local term for a small cart. He saw the events and heard a shout, so he went to the Softlys' pub and called out for Joe Lawton, then went to the place from whence the shout came. He saw the constable staggering, and helped him into the cart, which took the injured man to the police station.

Joseph Whitehead was another Birkenhead constable. He told the court that he remembered seeing the prisoner and Breen. PC Vaughan told him they had been causing a disturbance at the pub so he advised them again to go home. By this time both men were getting rather bad tempered, and started to cheek the police officers, PCs Whitehead and Vaughan. When asked his name, Smith said, 'I know and that's enough.'

The policemen were also getting impatient. Constable Whitehead grabbed Breen and held him, while PC Vaughan seized Smith by the collar of his jacket with his right hand. Vaughan had a stick in his hand but was not seen to use it. Smith said he would not go with PC Vaughan, who laid hold of him. What happened next was related by PC Whitehead:

> I saw Smith strike PC Vaughan several times in the left breast, and PC Vaughan shouted, 'I've been stabbed'. He let go Smith and fell. I then let go Breen, and called out to a constable named Clarke, whom I saw coming, to stop Smith. He did so. PC Vaughan came up to me, took off his belt and threw it with his stick to the ground. He said 'I am dying'. I went to fetch a surgeon, and then went to the place where Clarke knocked the prisoner down. There I found this diamond pointed knife, which I produce.

He showed the knife to the court; it was shut, but obviously a deadly weapon. 'I observed blood upon it. I saw a cut on the prisoner's hand,' he said, and continued his statement in stilted official language:

> I assisted to undress the deceased. I produce his great coat; there are four cuts in it. I also produce his vest and shirt. His shirt is saturated with blood. When the prisoner and his companion said they would not give their names, I said 'Then, let's take them to the Bridewell.' I let Breen go as soon as I heard the deceased was stabbed. Chester Street was not on PC Vaughan's beat that night. I had not been at a meeting that night.

As an example of the late officer's respectability, the court was told that Constable Vaughan was a member of the Orange Society.

Charles Clarke, a fellow Birkenhead policeman, also gave his statement:

I was on duty in Hamilton Street near Bridge Street. I heard a voice crying out, 'Stop him! Stop him – he has stabbed Vaughan!' I then met the prisoner running towards me. When within a few yards, he said with an oath, holding up his hand, 'Look out you.' I struck him on the top of his head, knocked him down and threw myself upon him. I then took him to the station. On the way he struggled violently twice, and I threw him on his back twice.

Mr Jeanette, a police surgeon, was sent to see to PC Vaughan. He told the court:

He was dying when I saw him. I helped to undress him and found a wound 2.5 inches in length below the left nipple, just below the sixth rib. It had passed over the sixth rib and entered the chest. After his death I made an examination of the body – the wound was 1.25 inches in depth, penetrating the apex of the heart. The knife produced might have caused the wounds which resulted in death. I also examined the prisoner. I found a cut above the second knuckle of his thumb on the right hand, and bruises on his back.

The prisoner's statement to the magistrates was then read out in court. He stated the facts already known, but added that when PC Vaughan came up to him the second time he struck him several times on the back and shoulder, and twisted his hand in his neckerchief; he then had no other way to defend himself but in the manner in which he did, but with no intention of killing the man.

Mr Morgan Lloyd then addressed the jury for the defence. He made great play of emphasising the point that the crucial element was malice aforethought. If a constable under a warrant was taking a man into custody, and was struck in such a way as to cause his death, then the crime would be murder. Had the prisoner any object in waylaying the deceased? No evidence. Had the deceased died doing his duty? Not proven – the deceased had not been on his regular beat at time of his killing. Mr Lloyd then went through the evidence, commenting on it as he proceeded, and urged the jury to consider the strong probability of the truth in his statement – that he had been drunk and had struck back in self-defence when hit on the back several times.

Mr Lloyd finished by referring to the defendant's previous good character – he was a sober, honest and industrious man, and was the only support of a widowed mother and five brothers and sisters. No man could have grieved over the result of this affair more than the prisoner himself. Smith proved this latter point by crying convulsively throughout the speech.

The judge summed up the trial after hearing more character witnesses. The judge said that there was no doubt that Smith had killed PC Vaughan. The point at issue was whether it was murder or manslaughter. Both involved killing people, but manslaughter was the crime of killing a man without malice aforethought. The authority with which the police constable was invested was obtained from the Birkenhead Improvement Act, the 3rd of William IV, cap 98, sec78 and read as follows:

That the said constable, assistant constables, watchmen, night patrols and beadles shall in their reversal courses of service use their utmost endeavours, not only to prevent fires, but also to keep watch and ward within the said townships, and to prevent murders &c; and they are hereby empowered and required to arrest and apprehend all malefactors, vagrants, beggars, disturbers of the peace, and all disorderly and suspected persons, prostitutes and night walkers, who shall be found misbehaving or wandering within the said township.

The deceased had relied upon the words 'disorderly or' disturbers of the peace'. Was the prisoner guilty of disturbing the peace at the time PC Vaughan made the arrest? If not, then the deceased had no lawful authority and the crime should be reduced to manslaughter and not murder. All the breach of the peace had ceased when PC Vaughan came up to Mrs Softly's house and therefore there had been no breach in his view, and in addition to this, Mrs Softly, who had witnessed the breach, refused to give the prisoner into custody for the offence.

The judge read over the witness statements, making comments as he went.

After deliberating for about a quarter of an hour, the jury returned with a verdict of guilty of manslaughter. The sentence was deferred until the next day.

The verdict was received with some slight cheers in the court, which were quickly subdued. The prisoner, who had been weeping throughout the trial, appeared greatly relieved by the verdict.

Though the judge had apparently been trying to save Smith's life by exposing loopholes the jury could use, he was not inclined to be lenient in his punishment. He told Smith that he had committed a serious crime, the manslaughter of an innocent man. There had been much violent crime in Cheshire recently, and an example had to be made. Therefore, he told Smith, he was imposing a sentence of transportation for fourteen years.

At this Smith left the dock, walking with a firm step into an uncertain future.

Chapter Twelve

⟫◇⟪

An Attempted Murder, 1861

It was a wet and miserable May morning in mid-Cheshire. Two people were up and about and on the road. They were on the tramp; wandering the roads without any permanent home, seeking work anywhere they could find it, though they were not very successful in finding any.

The man was 26-year-old Martin Doyle, who was younger than his partner. She was Jane Brogine, a married woman who had been cohabiting with Doyle for about a year. They tramped the countryside looking for work and handouts, a way of life of which Jane was getting tired. She wanted a home and a regular income. Apparently Jane was in bad mood that day. She told Doyle very firmly that he was to find work in Newcastle when they got there. Doyle was also in a foul mood. On that day, 30 May 1861, they were on the road, going on foot from Holmes Chapel to Newcastle-under-Lyme. They passed through the Linley Lane toll gate, then set down for a well-earned rest near Church Lawton. Seeking shelter from the cold drizzle, they found a hollow near the toll bar and under a tree. It seemed a good spot to shelter in, so they stayed there.

Jane complained of a headache, She put her head on Doyle's lap, and went to sleep, for, she later estimated, about an hour. She woke to find that Doyle's hand was pressing heavily on her head.

She told him to take it off – his heavy hand was worsening her headache and risked breaking her bonnet into a dozen pieces. He said nothing. He got up and went outside to see if it was still raining. He returned a short time later, about three minutes, with a large stone in his hand and others in his pockets. He threw the biggest stone at the right side of her head, knocking her unconscious. That was just the start of the battering. He next jumped on her chest and tried to strangle her around the neck, using enough force to cause her tongue to protrude out of her head. She screamed at him to spare her life, or at least give her a different death. She then prayed for mercy while Doyle cut her head with a sharp stone. She could feel the stone blade cutting into her head and face. She later told the court at Doyle's trial that she had cried out, 'Oh Dear me! My eyes are out of my head!' Doyle just grunted that he cared for

neither her eyes or her life. He then climbed on to her chest and said, 'Now, you b******, you are done! He then sat up, looked at her, and saw she was still breathing.

He jumped back on her chest as before, and shouted, 'You b******! What, are you not done yet?' He tried to finish the job by battering her head with such force that she started to drown in her own blood.

All the while he was saying, 'Jane, say no more, I intend to have your life; I came for it, and I will have it.' Then he hammered at her head again. When she appeared to be dead, he said, 'Now, b****** you, you are done right'. With that, he rose up from her chest and left. Jane collapsed. When she awoke from her faint, she was terrified that Doyle was still close by. She could hear nothing of him, but hearing a cart passing by, she shouted 'Man' as loud as she was able. The carter did not hear her. With what little strength she had, she crawled up the bank on her hands and knees. When she reached the top of the bank, the horrified carter saw her, and lifted her up onto his cart. He took the bloodstained and badly wounded woman to see a doctor and the police.

The police soon found Doyle. When arrested, there was no resistance or attempts at escape. He admitted his guilt.

Doyle said, 'You have no need to take hold of me, it was I that done it, and I am ready to suffer anything for it. The reason I did it was that she said if did not get work at Newcastle she should turn again.'

He confirmed Jane's account of the attack. They had been walking the lanes, wet and tired, until they found a place to rest. They both went to sleep. After the beating, he was sure she was dead, so he left her apparently lifeless corpse under a tree. He then went to the nearest brook to wash the blood off his hands. He then wandered around seeking a pond in which to drown himself.

A policeman went to the scene of the crime, where the relics of a violent assault were apparent. There was blood everywhere, and he found a woman's hair comb, and three stones which were covered in blood. These stones were picked up and taken to Doyle at his place of custody. Upon his arrival back at the station the constable was asked by Doyle, 'What have you got there? On being told the answer, he asked to take a look at them. He picked up a flattish, sharp stone out of the three, and said that that was the stone he had beaten her with. He knew for sure because when he was breaking her head, he had cut his hand on the sharp edge of that stone.

Meanwhile Jane was under medical care. Her surgeon found her in an awful state, exhausted from loss of blood. He was sure she would die from her injuries. He found many cuts and bruises about her person, especially on the head, face, hands and neck. All the cuts on the head had pierced through to the skull, laying bare the bone. Altogether, there were fourteen such cuts on her skull, and another seven or eight on the face. Her lower jawbone had been fractured. However the most serious wound was on the back of her head, a three inch long cut that had fractured her skull.

After a preliminary hearing at the local magistrates' court, Doyle was sent for trial at Chester Assizes.

The case opened on 8 August before Mr Justice Crompton, with Mr Latham prosecuting. Doyle was undefended by counsel, preferring to defend himself. The case attracted much attention locally. Even *The Times* had a representative at the trial. The *Times* man reported that this case was one of many such brutal cases with which this county unfortunately abounded. But this atrocity was the worst seen in many years. The courtroom, as was usual on such occasions, was crowded, mostly with 'women of all grades, ladies as well as others'.

Jane Brogine was brought into court to give evidence. At the bench, she seemed in a most dreadful state. Her face was seamed and scarred in a most dreadful manner, and a perfect thrill of horror ran through the court at her appearance. Appearing before the court meant reliving the terrible events of that May day. The experience was traumatic for poor Jane and, after a few minutes, she was taken so ill that she fainted. Her evidence stopped until she was given restoratives, and some water poured over her head to revive her.

During the cross-examination by the prosecution Jane fainted frequently, and uttered the most heart-rending moans. Doyle watched her with callous indifference.

The prosecution produced the stones which Doyle had used as a weapon. They were large and sharp, 'fit to fell an ox with'.

As he was defending himself, Doyle was allowed to cross-examine Jane himself. This he did at great length. He especially questioned her about why and how they had started the relationship, why she had left her husband, and what he coyly termed as 'a bad disease' with which she had in infected her husband. However, as the press reported, he did not ask her any question relevant to the matter in hand. He rambled on so wildly and vehemently that the judge had to stop his rantings several times. His violent language and demeanour caused poor Jane to collapse in a faint several times.

When he spoke to the jury, and the other witnesses, Doyle was perfectly calm and rational. However, his earlier vicious rant against Jane had probably lost him any sympathy the jury might have had. He addressed the jury 'at great length'. During this speech, he did reveal the reason why he hated her so much. He feared she had given him syphilis, then an incurable and usually fatal disease, producing a rash, scars, madness and ultimately death. Doyle also said Jane had attached herself to him, as she had been married to a much older man – a man so old, in fact, that she had said she was ashamed to be seen with him.

When questioning the doctor, Doyle asked him if he had found any traces of syphilis upon her. 'Yes,' the doctor said, though there was no trace of the disease upon Doyle. At the end of the day, the judge summed up the evidence for and against.

He took great care in going over the evidence, but stressed that it was the jury's task to determine the prisoner's intent when committing the crime. Did he or did he not intend to commit murder with malice aforethought? The jury retired for a few minutes, and then returned with a verdict of 'Guilty of wounding with intent to murder'.

Doyle was called forward to face the judge. Mr Justice Crompton said:

It is with great sorrow, but not without anxious deliberation, that I have come to the conclusion that I should not be doing my duty to the public if I did not pass sentence of death upon you. With the greatest deliberation you planned and committed the fearful act for which your life is now forfeited. You have awfully injured, and probably even yet fatally, the woman with whom you lived as your wife.

After describing the crime, he continued, 'I must now do my duty, and my duty is to sentence you to be hanged by the neck until you be dead, and may the Lord have mercy on your soul.'

The Times man agreed with the verdict, stating that it was a mere accident that Jane was not killed. The surgeon himself had said that nineteen out of twenty women would have been killed by the blows. The journalist went on to comment that, 'The way that women and even ladies sat out the filthy details necessarily elicited was anything but creditable to the sex.'

As for Doyle, he appeared a little penitent for a few days, but ten days before his execution he apparently became overcome with guilt. He admitted that he deserved to die, that he had been rightfully condemned, and that he welcomed death.

Despite his own submission to fate, others tried to save his life. A petition was drawn up and signed by some local citizens, calling for a commutation from death to life imprisonment. The Home Office declined the petition, and so the execution process started.

Doyle had a brother who, accompanied by Martin's legal wife, visited him in the condemned cell, but on neither occasion was there 'any extraordinary manifestation of feeling'.

Martin Doyle was executed in public a few days later, on the morning of 27 August 1861.

Following the usual Cheshire practice, on hanging day he was transferred from county to city jurisdiction at the Glover Stone. There was a great crowd and a strong parapet had to be erected in order to contain the eager spectators.

His executioner was the most famous English hangman of the century, William Calcraft. Calcraft was a kindly man who enjoyed the company of his children, grandchildren, and his pets. Despite his personal kindness, his method of execution was cruel. He employed the 'short drop' in which the victim often slowly strangled to death rather than be killed quickly. He began his career in 1829, as the London city executioner. Employed at Horsemonger Lane Gaol in Surrey, he would have hanged the Ashton murderers in 1834, and possibly poor Mary Gallop, who suffered slow strangulation at her execution. Calcraft was also the flogger in chief, being paid to carry out birchings on petty criminals – half a crown a time. The public hangman had a well-paid job. He had regular stipend from the London authorities of one guinea a week, plus one guinea per execution. Calcraft was able to perform provincial executions for a fee of £10 per execution.

Doyle's execution was an historic event in that it was one of the last public executions to be carried out in Chester. Public executions were banned under the Capital Punishment Amendment Act of 1868. Doyle's death was also the final execution for attempted murder in England.

Chapter Thirteen

⟫◆⟪

Captain Beswick, 1869

Major Frederick Beswick was the chief of police and fire services in Birkenhead. He expected a visit from the City of London Police, regarding a fraud case. The expected visitor from London arrived, a Sergeant Webb and his assistant, Detective Sergeant Skate of the Liverpool Police. They came to see the respectable Major about an attempted fraud on the Bank of England. As Major Beswick expected, they served the warrant for fraud upon the suspect – him. The next day, Monday, 10 May 1869, Major Beswick appeared at a preliminary hearing before the Lord Mayor of London at the Justice Room of the Mansion House in London.

Quite how and why he found himself in such a predicament is a long and complex story. Frederick Beswick was born in the north of England, at Buxton, in 1818. He joined the army in 1836, entering the 38th Foot as a private. He was an industrious, able and ambitious soldier, and worked his way up through the non-commissioned ranks. By 1849 he was an Ensign – the lowest commissioned officer rank. The term was abolished in 1871, and the rank was renamed to that of Second Lieutenant. The Crimean War broke out in October 1853. As a serving soldier, Beswick was sent to Russia, where he fought and was wounded at the battles of the Alma River (September 1854), and Inkerman, in November 1854. On 29 December that year he received another promotion, perhaps a battlefield one, when he was given his captaincy 'without purchase' – in other words on merit. When he arrived back in England, after the war, the then Captain Beswick of the 38th was presented with his Crimean War medal by Queen Victoria herself. He was one of many hundreds of servicemen who received the honour at a great 'Welcome Home' celebration in London in May 1855.

After the Crimean War, Beswick became Adjutant of the Depot Battalion 'vice Nelson' on 9 February 1855. In 1863 he was on half pay, serving in the 5th Lancers, but became a Major at their Depot on 28 July 1863. In 1865 he sold his commission and went into civilian life. That same year his first child – a daughter named Maud – was born.

While in the army, he had been stationed in Gibraltar for some years from 1840. During that time he made friends with a Henry T. Maxted, and married Elizabeth

An unknown Captain of the 38th Foot. The emblem on the cap is the 'Staffordshire Knot'. The regiment recruited in the county and later became the Staffordshire Regiment.

Lobb, on 23 April 1844. It was also in Gibraltar that he set in motion the events that were to lead to his disgrace.

On his way back to England from the Crimea, in 1856, he had spent a happy day with his old friend, Henry T. Maxted. Maxted had been appointed a Trustee in the will of a prominent local businesswoman, Miss Agnes Cundy. After some small legacies were given, a total of £4,500 was left to be invested in Consols (fixed interest Government securities). Income from these funds was to be given to Miss Cundy's various relatives – her brother, sister and niece. The necessary arrangements for collecting and distributing the funds was the responsibility of the two Trustees, Mr Maxted and a Mr Joseph Underwood.

In Victorian times, the police and fire services were one, so when Beswick became Chief Constable he became responsible for dealing with all crimes and fires. One of his first duties was to attend to a burning ship, the *Samuel Cearns*, which, loaded with flammable materials – jute, cotton, and so on – had burst into flame upon arrival in the Mersey. It was thought that the fire was caused by the spontaneous combustion of the jute on board. Major Beswick and his police and fire teams were prompt and courageous in action. They managed to save all the crew and some of the cargo. The event reached the national newspapers and led to great praise for Major Beswick and his force. His other actions whilst in charge were also efficient and honourable. He became greatly trusted by all.

In 1867 Mr Underwood died, and Major Beswick was selected to replace him as Trustee to Miss Cundy's will. In that same year, the terms of the will changed due to the death of one of the annuitants, a Mr Cundy. The dead man left part of his share of the funds to another relative. The remaining funds amounted to £4,216 13s 4d, which was invested in the name of both Trustees – Mr Maxted and Major Beswick. These funds could not be used by the Trustees for personal use. Any withdrawal had to be agreed by both men, and the required documentation signed by them both. As Major Beswick was in Birkenhead, and Mr Maxted was in Gibraltar, that meant the funds were unlikely to be drawn upon by either.

The interest from the funds was paid into the Birkenhead branch of the Alliance Bank, who then distributed the monies to the relatives.

The charge against Major Beswick was that of illegally drawing from the account the sum of £400. The tale outlined in court was that Major Beswick had gone to the Alliance Bank in Birkenhead on 26 January 1868. He called upon the branch manager, a Mr Hinde, and told him that £400 was to be paid out of Trust Funds. This was because Mr Maxted had sent him a letter stating that he was going to California, and would pass through Liverpool on his way to America. Major Beswick said he had been asked to gain the power of attorney, i.e. authorisation to withdraw money from the account on his signature alone. Mr Maxted would confirm the arrangements when he arrived in Liverpool. All Major Beswick had to do was to ask the bank to obtain power of attorney from the Bank of England, to allow the deal to go through.

After some correspondence between all the English parties involved, a power of attorney was granted by the Bank of England, allowing the withdrawal of £400 cash, or £431 in Consols, from the Trust Fund into the Alliance Bank on 2 February 1868. The letter of authorisation was sent to Birkenhead the same day. The very next day, Mr Hinde the bank manager said that he saw Major Beswick with the authorisation letter. The Alliance Bank also that day, 3 February, sent a letter to Mr Maxted stating that they had, in accordance with his wishes, given Major Beswick the power of attorney he had asked for. A similar formal letter was sent to Major Beswick, who wrote to Mr Maxted a letter stating that he had asked for the power of attorney, as he wanted to make better use of Miss Cundy's money. Indeed, he had said in his letter that he had often thought that the monies were badly invested in the Three Per Cent Consols. They could and should be put into higher yielding funds, especially as two of the annuitants, who he named, were now in greatly reduced circumstances. However, as any decision required the agreement of both men, he wished to know the opinion of Mr Maxted, as soon as possible, as exciting opportunities were opening up every day in Merseyside. Finally, wrote Major Beswick, he would like Mr Maxted to know that he would do everything in his power to help the Cundy family.

The letter and bank notice from Birkenhead arrived in Gibraltar by 15 February. Mr Maxted wrote to Major Beswick, pointing out that Miss Cundy had had many opportunities, whilst in business, to invest in properties paying a guaranteed five per cent or over. However, she had no confidence in any investment apart from British Government securities. The income from these investments went to her family and, in respect of her wishes, he declined to make any alteration in the investments. He also wrote to the Bank of England to stop any further proceedings in the proposed transfer. However, a few days later, 23 February, Major Beswick took his power of attorney to Mr Hinde, the Birkenhead bank manager. The document was supposedly signed by both the Major and Mr Maxted, and witnessed by Lieutenant Colonel Twibill and Mr John Chandler, friends and employees of Major Beswick.

In the document, Mr Maxted was described as 'of Gibraltar', but Mr Hinde suggested that the words 'late of Gibraltar' would be more accurate, and should be inserted. Major Beswick agreed, so he went away, returning a little later with the necessary correction. He said this had been done by Mr Maxted, a house guest at Major Beswick's home in Woodside. The document was then sent to London, and stopped by the Bank of England. Inquiries began to be made. The Bank of England informed Mr Hinde of their suspicions. Upon receipt of the letter, on 26 February, Mr Hinde went that evening to see Major Beswick. Beswick assured Mr Hinde that he had put forward the proposal for power of attorney entirely in good faith.

Soon after, on 1 March, Major Beswick wrote to Maxted in Gibraltar, asking to know by return of post whether any person resembling him (Beswick) had left Gibraltar recently, or who knew his writing and could imitate it, or who knew of his (Beswick's) connections with the Cundy family. If the answer was positive, would Mr Maxted let him have at once a full description of name and person, as 'most vile attempt at imposition' had been made upon him. This had only been foiled by Mr Beswick's return from the countryside. He added that he had reason to believe the 'fellowship still in Liverpool'. Furthermore, Major Beswick added, he was in full pursuit of the villain. He had set two of his best detectives on the case.

Mr Maxted wrote back promptly, stating that he was surprised by this request. He could not recall anyone in Gibraltar who both resembled Major Beswick and had left the Rock recently. Nor did he know anyone who knew how the Cundy monies had been invested. From Mr Hinde and Mr Maxted the Bank of England had enough information to suspect that a major fraud was under way. So they started more inquiries, as a result of which Mr Maxted was brought from Gibraltar. He arrived in London on a Saturday morning, and made a sworn statement before a court. As a consequence of that action, a warrant was granted, to be delivered by Sergeant Webb of the City of London Police detective branch, 'a most efficient officer' who immediately went to Birkenhead, arriving in the evening at Major Beswick's house in Woodside.

This brings us back to the Monday morning in the Mansion House Court, where Major Beswick was having an uncomfortable time. The prosecuting counsel, a Mr Freshfield, said he had the honour to appear for the Governor and Company of the Bank of England. The bank regretted very much the course they had had to take, having regard for the prisoner's position and family, but he was sure that the court would agree that they had no alternative. The witnesses were then called.

Mr Maxted gave his evidence to the hearing. He stated that he was resident in Gibraltar, where he was Treasurer to the Sanitary Commissioners, and clerk to the garrison's quartermaster. He confirmed that the amount in Miss Cundy's name was £4,216 13s 4d as of February 1868. He then said that he had never written to Major Beswick (he referred to his old friend as 'the prisoner') informing him that:

I was coming to England or going to the United States, and would call upon him at Liverpool. I never had any communication with him about the power of attorney to transfer the sum of £431 5s 3d from the Trust Fund. I never concurred in or in any way directed such a sale.

He went to say that he had received the letter from Major Beswick, and the details from the Bank of England, on the same day. He wrote back to the bank saying he had not sanctioned any such transfer. Furthermore,

> the power of attorney document, supposedly signed by me, was not so signed, I had not authorised anyone to sign it for me. I did not apply to the bank for such a document, and I was not at Woodside, Birkenhead, at the time the document was signed. At that time I was in Gibraltar.

In fact, said Mr Maxted, until brought over by the bank, Major Beswick had never been to England in his life.

Major Beswick's confidential clerk (private secretary) was then brought forward to testify. He said that some time previously he had been asked to sign a document given to him by Major Beswick. The signing may have been in the Major's office or a side room – he could not remember which. However, there was no other signatory present.

Major Beswick's defence lawyer, Mr Wontner, told the court that his client was a man well-known and respected in Birkenhead. Enquiries were still ongoing in that town. There were many people willing to testify to the Major's honesty and integrity. Though granted a power of attorney, it took 21 days before the Major acted upon it. He knew that in that period Mr Maxted would be contacted by the bank. Could anyone have contemplated a fraud, knowing that it would be discovered and denounced by Mr Maxted? The two signatories were Colonel Twibill and Mr Chandler, both of whom could be contacted at any moment. 'There was such an absence of secrecy in the transaction as to be utterly irreconcilable with a guilty intent.' Mr Wotner continued that the only reasonable explanation was that the good Major had been swindled by someone impersonating Mr Maxted. Finally, he had known for some six weeks that enquiries were being made by the Bank of England. He had not attempted to flee; in fact, when arrested, he was still in his post. Were these the actions of a guilty man? At the very least, Major Beswick deserved bail. Mr Freshfield, for the bank, heard his arguments, and then said that the case was so serious that the bank could not, and would not, consent to bail being allowed. The Lord Mayor agreed, and remanded Major Beswick in jail.

At the later hearing, before the Lord Mayor of London, detective Henry Webb said he had met Major Beswick, and told him he had a warrant. He offered to read it to Major Beswick, who replied that he knew what was in it, and had been expecting to be charged, as he had been aware of the Bank of England's enquiries for the last two months. Major Beswick had told him that he had only done the deed out of kindness to the supposed Mr Maxted. If he had been guilty of deliberately forging a document, he would have fled along ago, but he was determined to 'stand it'. Sergeant Webb and his Liverpool assistant had searched Major Beswick's office, and found the deed of 1867, appointing new Trustees, a copy of Miss Cundy's will, his Alliance Bank passbook, several letters from Mr Maxted, and a printed handbill, offering a reward of £20 for the arrest of the man who was alleged to have impersonated Mr Maxted. The reward was never claimed.

Major Beswick was committed to stand trial at Newgate. The trial opened before Mr Justice Pigott on Wednesday 8 June. Well-dressed Major Beswick made a contrast to the usual clientele of the court – petty criminals and prostitutes.

The prosecution case was that early in 1869, Major Beswick had fallen into financial difficulties. The bank authorities had been very diligent in investigating his financial affairs. Some of his creditors were 'clamorous', but there was only £11 in his account at the Alliance Bank. So, continued the prosecution, the Major had the idea that if he could borrow some money from the Trust Fund, paying what would have been the dividend upon it, and then reinvest the 'borrowed' sum when in funds, then no harm would be done, and nobody would notice. He was desperate, as his bills amounted to £370. A sum of £400 would cover his bills, the dividend payment, and leave a little over. He was reported to have told one creditor, a grocer, that he would pay his £50 bill when he sold some stock, which he would do shortly.

The defence made much of Major Beswick's reputation – 'he had fought and bled at the Alma and Inkerman', and the fact that the forged signature bore no resemblance to Major Beswick's handwriting, so there could have been an impersonator. But, if there was, he was never detected.

Mr Baron Pigott summed up for the jury, who retired for an hour. They returned with a verdict of Guilty, but with a recommendation for mercy with regard to the prisoner's previous good character and large family. Mr Baron Pigott addressed him, saying that it was with extreme pain that he had to pass judgement upon such a person as he, in his station in life. 'But this was a crime that could not be passed over lightly.' He then sentenced Major Beswick to five years penal servitude.

In 1871 he was at Gillingham Prison in Kent. His first wife had died. However, by 1874 he must have been released from jail as he was able to marry again. His second wife was Ellan Kearvell (1846-1919). The couple retired to Bathwick in Somerset, a place which is now the BA2 area of Bath City. By 1881 he was listed in the Census as 'Retired Major', but had changed his name to Edgerton. He died of consumption in 1882. His widow survived him by many years.

Chapter Fourteen

———⟫•◇•⟪———

The Gorse Hall Murder, 1909

The Gorse Hall murder has appeared in print many times. My excuse for including it here is that it is impossible to mention Cheshire crimes without giving details of one of Britain's most unusual, and still unsolved, cases.

In the autumn of 1909, George Harry Storrs was 49 years old, around 6ft tall, and apparently happily married. He lived in a grand house, Gorse Hall, in east Cheshire. The Hall was the second mansion on the site, and a suitable home for a wealthy man and his family. Storrs' father had purchased the 1830s building as a wedding present for his son in 1891.

It was on a site between Stalybridge and Dukinfield, overlooking the moors and road to Lancashire and Yorkshire. It was on Hough Hill. Gorse Hall was a dreary, stone-built pile surrounded by dense shrubbery. Storrs had not made his fortune by spending money. His house was bereft of electricity, gas and telephones. It was lit only by candles and oil lamps.

The house was in the Dukinfield Police area, the grounds in the Stalybridge area. Dukinfield Police were a division of the Cheshire Constabulary, while Stalybridge was a borough force, not becoming part of the Cheshire Constabulary until the 1940s.

The place had been empty for a few years before the Storrs moved in. George had a small family – himself, his wife, his niece Miss Marion Lindley, who lived with Mr and Mrs Storrs as an adopted daughter, and a small staff – there were no children, though George was close to his nephews and nieces. In 1909 his staff comprised James Worrall, coachman, and his wife Sarah. They had joined the staff in 1903. There were also two others: cook Mary Emily Evans and housemaid Eliza Cooper. Though described in some reports as a mill owner, contemporary accounts state that Storrs was also a builder. In fact, his family were prominent in many local business and political circles – his brother James was a local Justice of the Peace.

Though he had wealth, respect and good health, Storrs was a worried man. Strange events had been occurring throughout the autumn of 1909.

On 10 September, an intruder had come to the front window of the house when the family were having dinner. The man waved a gun and was heard to shout, 'Hands up or I fire!' A pane of glass was broken, and, said the family, two shots were fired. George Storrs was a brave man with a short temper – he ran out of the house to confront the gunman – who had fled into the night.

The Dukinfield Police soon arrived, but found nothing that night. A more detailed examination the next morning revealed no signs of forced entry, apart from the broken window pane, and no signs of bullet holes in the dining room.

After that incident, Storrs wrote a list of those he suspected were behind the attack – but the list had only two names upon it. He also requested police protection – the police promised to step-up patrols in the area. A policeman was also assigned to patrol the grounds every night, as part of his regular beat. Furthermore, a bell was installed on the roof – this would be rung whenever there was a threat to the house. However, some sources say that Storrs rang the bell frequently, and these false alarms upset the police. The Hall was on a small hill, approached up a steep and slippery lane, and the police did not like walking and slipping up the lane for false alarms. However, they did their duty. That is, however, until early November.

On 1 November there was an election. All available police officers were in town keeping order amongst the crowds. There were no police officers to spare for the patrols of Gorse Hall. Not that the Storrs seemed worried. That night they were in the dining room awaiting their supper. At about 9 p.m. (some reports say 9.30 p.m.) that night, the cook went into the cellar to fetch some milk. Coming up the stairs, she saw a man outside, at the kitchen door, and thought it was James Worrall, the coachman. 'Oh, Worrall, you gave me a fright,' she said – then realised it was not Worrall standing there. The stranger pointed a gun at her and growled, 'Speak, and I shoot!' She fled screaming into the dining room. Mrs Storrs, as formidable as her husband, grabbed a weapon displayed on the wall: an Irish shillelagh, a thick heavy stick with a knob on the end. With this she was able to knock the pistol out of the intruder's hand. Mrs Storrs ran upstairs to ring the alarm bell, kicking the gun under a carpet as she went. Meanwhile, Mr Storrs grabbed the man and a struggle ensued. The intruder said, 'Now I have got you!' as he drew a knife from his clothing and began to stab Mr Storrs with it.

Marion Lindley ran down the drive towards Albert Square. As she went, the sound of the alarm bell sounded, as Mrs Storrs rang it. Miss Lindley fled into Stalybridge. She ran into the Liberal Club and managed to tell the steward that something was happening at Gorse Hall. The steward politely said that the club was open to men only, and directed her to the Oddfellows Hall. Arriving there, Marion could only whisper, 'They are murdering my uncle!'

Two men took her back to the Liberal Club, where the steward settled her in a back room with a glass of brandy. The steward had rung the police, who were on the way to Gorse Hall. At the inquest, on 10 November, Mr Harry Heald said he was in the Central Liberal Club that night, and heard talk of a fire or commotion at Gorse Hall,

The scene of the murder. A newspaper sketch of the kitchen where Mr Storrs was stabbed. (Courtesy of Tameside Local Studies and Archives Centre)

as they could hear the alarm bell being rung. So he and many others made their way to the Hall, where they found a terrible scene in the kitchen.

Mr Storrs was still alive, but barely so. At a later trial, the pathologist said he had suffered fifteen wounds, to his head, hands and neck, from a thin sharp knife: 'the wounds could have been inflicted within two minutes with such a weapon.'

Storrs was still conscious, so Heald asked him the obvious question, who had done it? Storrs just moaned, 'Oh my back,' and called for his wife. He was, said Heald, obviously in great pain. However, another of the Liberal Club party, an electrician, Mr Joseph Knott, was sure that he heard Storrs moan, in answer to the question, 'I don't know – they have escaped.'

PC Buckley said he arrived at the house about 9.15 p.m., to be told by a maid about Mr Storrs.

Mrs Storrs was still upstairs, ringing the alarm bell – it took two strong men to pull her away from the bell rope.

The police investigation started by taking fingerprints from the windows, though they were not used in evidence in the subsequent trials. The Hall's horse trough was examined. There were clots of blood floating in it, as though someone had tried to wash away bloodstains. Around the trough were boot marks, and the police took a plaster cast of them. Neither clue proved useful. The blood clots were identified as pond weed. Storrs had no known deadly enemies. Unlike the unfortunate Mr Ashton eighty years earlier, there were no murderous Unionists wanting to kill him. Industrial relations were harmonious. His business colleagues and rivals respected him, and had no motive or desire to kill him. The police found and followed up on Storrs' list of enemies – neither man fitted the description of the attacker. He was described as a young man, 25 to 27 years of age, height 5ft 6ins to 5ft 8ins, thin featured, a fair to pale

The funeral of Mr Storrs. The photograph was probably taken near Trinity Street Stalybridge. (Courtesy of Tameside Local Studies and Archives Centre)

complexion, a slight fair moustache, wearing a cap and tweed suit' with the appearance 'of a working man'. The intruder's revolver was found to be fake, a useless dummy revolver. It had once been a proper gun, but was now deactivated.

Mr Storrs was buried 10 November. His coffin was carried to Saint Paul's Church, Stalybridge, in a hearse drawn by two black horses. Behind it were twenty horse-drawn coaches of mourners. Along the route, all house blinds were drawn as a mark of respect. The day after the funeral of Storrs, his faithful servant, James Worrall, told the other staff that he was going out shopping. He did not come back, so at a late hour they started searching for him. He was found hanging from a beam in the stables.

The police had a clue to the murder. Someone had mentioned the name of Cornelius Howard, a local man. His description was issued. Apart from being 31 instead of in his mid-twenties, his description fitted that of the murderer. A few days later in nearby Oldham, a man was arrested on a charge of burglary. He gave his name as John Ward but he was soon identified as Cornelius Howard. He was the wanted man. And he was a cousin of G.H. Storrs.

Cornelius Howard was the black sheep of the family. His father had been a pork butcher in Dukinfield. Cornelius had joined the family business, but had left for a life of petty crime. In 1901 he enlisted, entering the Royal Field Artillery where served in India and rose to the rank of Bombardier (corporal). He left the regular army at Woolwich in April 1909. Since his return to civilian life, he had returned to crime. Suspicion was further aroused by his injuries – he had bloodstains on his clothes, and bruises on his left side. The Oldham police sent him to Dukinfield police station in a motor car. There, Miss Lindley and two servants identified him as the man who had intruded on 1 November. A special court was soon constituted. At this preliminary

Police Detective Inspector Albert Lee with his wife and son outside the family home 'Honeymoon Row', Cambridge Terrace, Millbrook. Inspector Lee was the officer who cut down the body of John Worrall, the coachman. (Courtesy of Tameside Local Studies and Archives Centre)

hearing, Howard said nothing. His defence counsel stated that Howard had been in Huddersfield on the night in question. In fact, the Ring O' Bells pub, where he was playing against the landlord and others in a domino match for half a gallon of beer. The prosecution claimed that the domino match had taken place the next day, 2 November. The Cheshire County Analyst said he had found traces of blood, fat and grease on the knife found on Howard. A Mrs Doolan, of Joyce's Lodging House, Oldham said that Howard had entered her premises at 11 p.m. She did not say anything about his appearance, apart from his fair moustache. There was no mention of bloodstains on his clothing. He was remanded in custody by the magistrate, for trial at Chester Assizes on a charge of murder. The police soon discovered that he was certainly not the man responsible for the attack on Gorse Hall on 10 September. He had the perfect alibi – at the time he was in Wakefield Gaol serving a sentence for shop breaking.

He was tried at Chester Assizes in March 1910. He had an explanation for his injuries – he had received them whilst burgling the premises of Messrs Tansey & Walker of Stalybridge. The main evidence against him was that of the Gorse Hall ladies, who had all identified him as the intruder. But, there were few other facts against him.

Mrs Storrs had broken down in tears at the magistrates' court when she pointed to Howard as the intruder. However, at the Dukinfield police station line-up, she had pointed out another man. There was no apparent motive, no clinching evidence such as fingerprints, blood-soaked clothing, no connection with the revolver found at the scene. The only evidence was that of Mrs Storrs, Marion Lindley, Mary Emily Evans and the housemaid Eliza Cooper.

In the final summing up, the defence counsel, Trevor Lloyd, pointed out that the ladies' evidence was the only serious case against Howard. There was no other evidence, no motive to condemn his client. If the two events of September and November were linked, then Howard was innocent as he had a perfect alibi for 10 September.

The prosecution counsel could only remind the jury of the identification evidence. The jury retired for twenty minutes, before returning with a verdict of 'Not Guilty'. The court exploded with glee, as the public gallery cheered and shouted. The judge, Mr Justice Pickford, told them to be quiet, and then said, 'Now that you have ceased that indecent exhibition, I can go on to order the prisoner to be discharged. You ought to be ashamed of yourselves, not knowing bow to behave in a Court of Justice.' Howard left the dock, and walked outside the court to be met by a cheering crowd.

And there matters lay until the summer of 1910.

In June, a courting couple reported an assault on them. James Bolton and Gertrude Booth were walking arm-in-arm along Early Bank Road during the late evening of Monday 20 June. At 10 p.m. they started for home. They barely noticed a muttering young man, until he grabbed Gertrude by the neck and yelled, 'Do what I want, or I'll cut your throat!'

James Bolton promptly fought the man, freeing Gertrude, telling her to run; 'He's got knife!' She did. The fight continued for four or five minutes. The attacker stabbed James then ran away. The couple went straight to Dukinfield police station and gave an account of the incident and a description of the attacker: light hair, 25 to 30 years old, about 5ft 8ins in height. Inspector William Brewster recognised that description – it was the same as that of the Gorse Hall attacker. On Thursday 23 June the police arrested a local man, Mark Wilde, of 48 Robinson Street, Stalybridge. He lived with his parents and, like Cornelius Howard, he was an ex-soldier who had served abroad.

The police questioned him about the incidents at Gorse Hall and Early Bank Road. For the Gorse Hall events, Wilde admitted that he had not gone to his work on the nightshift of 10 September 1909. Instead, he claimed to have been drinking all night in the Astley Arms, the pub opposite his parents' house. As for the night of 1 November, he had again been drinking, in three pubs in town. On his way home he was involved in a fight, a fierce one. He arrived home with his shirt and jacket covered in bloodstains. The police obtained the clothes he claimed to have worn in November. He also claimed to own two pistols, relics of his service days. One was an 'American Bullock', the same make as the one dropped by the intruder at Gorse Hall.

Wilde stood trial for the Early Bank assault in July. He told the court that he had made three statements to the police. Inspector Brewster told the court that two of those statements referred to 'another matter'. Wilde was identified as the Early Bank attacker by the courting couple, and a local man, George Hayes, who knew him. Hayes said that he had seen Wilde on 20 June, looking as if he had been in a fight and with something shiny up his sleeves. The knife had been found discarded near Wilde's home. Wilde denied the knife was his and denied attacking the courting couple, but did admit to seeing George Hayes on that evening. Wilde received a two month prison sentence, to be served in Knutsford Gaol. Whilst he was in custody, police work continued on the Storrs murder.

Mrs Storrs had moved to Harrogate, taking Mary Emily Evans, her cook, with her. Mrs Storrs later moved to another stone-built pile in the Morecambe Bay area. She ordered that Gorse Hall be destroyed, and with it all her unpleasant memories. Before calling in the demolition gang, she moved all her prized possessions to her new home, and invited locals to take from Gorse Hall anything they wanted. The locals took her at her word, even taking the decorative doorknobs.

Called back to Cheshire for an identity parade, she and Marion were unsure about Wilde's identity, though the two servants were positive that he was the man who had invaded Gorse Hall. Wilde left Knutsford Goal, only to be promptly rearrested and charged with the murder of Mr Storrs.

The case opened on 24 October at Chester Castle, with Mr Justice Horridge as the presiding judge. There were two lawyers for the Crown, Mr R. Francis Williams QC and Mr Ellis Griffith MP. For the prisoner was Mr Edward T. Nelson, the son of Guyanese parents, and quite possibly the first West Indian barrister in Britain.

The prosecution case was outlined. The prisoner, Mark Wilde, was an ex-soldier whose appearance resembled that of witness statements in the Gorse Hall murder. Three former Army associates would testify that the revolver found at Gorse Hall was one which the prisoner had in his possession when he left the army at the beginning of 1909. Proof would be given that clothes worn on 1 November were bloodstained. Witnesses would testify that Wilde was the intruder of 1 November. The witnesses were the widow Storrs and her servants. Mr Nelson found and worked on two weak points. These were the confused witness identifications and the lack of any clinching evidence, such as bloodstains or fingerprints.

Mary Emily Evans, the cook formerly employed at Gorse Hall, had picked the prisoner out from a line-up in Knutsford Gaol from thirteen others on 23 August. When cross-examined, she admitted she could not swear that he was the man she had seen that night in November, but could say that he resembled the man. Mrs Storrs broke down under fierce cross-examination, sobbing, 'Haven't I lived a lifetime since November last? You forget, Mr Nelson, all that I have gone through.' Marion said she was positive in her identification, but agreed that she had been equally as sure of Howard's identity at the previous murder trial.

Dr William Henry Wilcox, senior Home Office analyst, said he had examined Wilde's clothing and found traces of blood – human blood – on the prisoner's clothes. He was then given leave to return to London, where he was to be a witness in the trial of Ethel Le Neve, Dr Crippen's lady friend.

The prosecution line of attack continued with evidence about the gun left at Gorse Hall. The gun in question was an 'American Bullock' of .32 calibre, made in Belgium. They were cheap copies of the 'American Bulldog' type, itself a copy of the famed

Police officers outside Dukinfield police station. (Courtesy of Tameside Local Studies and Archives Centre)

Webley & Scott 'British Bulldog' of 1878. All these guns were short-barrelled pistols, designed to be hidden in a coat pocket or handbag. They fired gunpowder cartridges instead of the more powerful cordite charges. They fired heavy bullets a short range – the classic 'Bulldog' had a .44 bullet – and at short range they were lethal – American President Garfield was killed with an 'American Bulldog' in 1881.

The prosecution brought forth a witness from Wilde's army days. He had served in Malta with the Worcestershire Regiment. A fellow soldier, now a policeman, Samuel Charles Wellings of the Liverpool Police, testified that he had seen the Gorse Hall gun in Wilde's luggage when returning home to England. He described the gun's faults, markings and decorations exactly. Another fellow soldier, Frank Fowles, also said he had seen the gun in Wilde's possession. A gunsmith, Mr Pickford, told how he had examined the bullet jammed in the chamber of the Gorse Hall gun, and compared it to a bullet found at Wilde's home. The two bullets were almost identical.

The defence produced a new witness – Cornelius Howard. He had put on weight since his trial, but stood next to Wilde in the court to show how similar they were. If the witnesses were mistaken in identifying him, surely they could also be wrong in identifying Wilde?

Mark Wilde had no alibi for the night of 10 September. He had found work as a shunter at Stalybridge station. However, that night he did not turn up for work, and was sacked. He repeated his claim that he had spent that night in the Astley Arms.

As for 1 November, Wilde said that he had knocked against a man in the street outside a pub, and got into a fight. Despite the publicity surrounding the case, no one came forward to admit being the other man, no one saw Wilde either fighting or walking around bloodstained, and no one saw him drinking in a pub at the time of the murder.

Wilde said he was told of the murder by his cousin, Thomas Lockwood, later that night. When Wilde returned home, his mother noticed blood on his clothes. Fearing that he might be accused of involvement in the Storrs murder, Mrs Wilde persuaded her son to destroy his pistols. This he did by dismantling them and chucking the parts away in local ponds and canals. The bits were never found. However, witnesses – friends of the Wildes – were produced to testify that they had seen Wilde's pistols on his mantelpiece a few weeks after the murder.

Mr Nelson, for the defence, summed up by stressing that the if witnesses were wrong in the first trial – were they right now? He also made the crucial point that the murderer would have been drenched in blood; it would have been all over his outerwear, underwear, trousers and shoes. No blood was found on Wilde's trousers, only superficial blood on his coat and shirt.

The jury retired for twenty minutes before returning with a verdict of 'Not Guilty'. The astonished judge could only say, 'Mark Wilde, you are discharged.' Wilde left the court to return to Dukinfield, and then into respectable obscurity.

Cornelius Howard became a clerk in Blackpool, and rejoined the army in the First World War. He survived the conflict. Maggie Storrs retired to Morecambe Bay, where she died in 1926. Marion Lindley married a society doctor, who later turned to drink. Her only son followed his father's dissolute ways until he joined the army in the Second World War. He died in the Normandy landings. Marion herself lived until 1960.

Theories about 'whodunnit' are numerous. One popular suggestion is that Mr Storrs had done wrong to a Continental girl who committed suicide. The theory is that her relatives came to England to kill him in revenge. In 2008 a local author, Barry Sullivan, developed a new theory. He noticed that another local murderer was identical in description to that of the Gorse Hall intruder. He was a local carter, Alfred Derrick, who stabbed his fiancée to death in the summer of 1910. Condemned to death, he was reprieved.

But, a century later, we still know no more than Mr Storrs about who stabbed him.

Chapter Fifteen

⇒◆⇐

The Calladine Case, 1923

Hannah Calladine lived in Nantwich. Originally from Chesterfield in Derbyshire, she and her family had moved to Nantwich during the First World War. Hannah worked in local clothing factories that were busy with orders from the armed forces. Hannah met a man from Chesterfield, Albert Edward Burrows, who was then in his fifties. He wooed her, he had a child by her, and he probably talked about their future together. What he did not tell her was that he was already married, with a wife and family in Glossop. Unable or unwilling to pay, Hannah sued him for maintenance of his child, and he served a short time in jail for non-payment. Afterwards, he and Hannah moved to Glossop. After a few months there, Hannah's family lost contact with her. They placed advertisements in Cheshire and Derbyshire newspapers begging her, or anyone who knew her, to make contact. No replies came. The reason why was revealed in 1923.

Burrows had settled in Glossop with his former wife. Next door lived the Wood family. Burrows was in the habit of taking their son, Tommy, for walks in the countryside. On Sunday, 4 March 1923, the two went out over the moors. Only one came back. Burrows told Mr Wood that little Tommy was missing and volunteered for the search party. He also told people, 'If you see little Tommy, send him home.' Suspicion soon fell upon Burrows. He fled across the moors, but was found hiding under a holly bush by a Mr Ambrey. Burrows allegedly told Ambrey, 'I don't know what made me do it,' and he 'would not be like Charlie Peace and tremble on the scaffold.' (Peace was a notorious Victorian criminal executed by William Marwood in 1879.)

Little Tommy's body was found stuffed down an airshaft at a disused mine. At the inquest, Mr Nicholson, Chief Inspector of Mines, said that the airshaft had been secured properly. There was no possibility of Tommy falling in by accident. The coroner's jury retired at 8.08, and returned at 8.45 with a verdict of 'Wilful Murder'. Burrows did not speak, but there was clapping in court. Burrows was taken away by car, on remand, the police car followed by a large and hostile crowd.

High Sreet, Glossop, c. 1910.

On 5 April, Albert Edward Burrows was formally charged with the murder of 3-year-old Tommy Wood. A hostile crowd awaited the arrival of the prisoner at the railway station (Derby) as he was driven to the court in a closed van. He was remanded in custody at Strangeways Prison in Manchester. Whilst there, he was in the hospital wing. He made some remarks to a fellow prisoner that aroused police suspicions. There could be more bodies down the shaft.

In May the search began. It could have been a wild goose chase – the police had few definite leads, only a strong suspicion. On 23 May, a further search of the pit shaft at Simmondley began, for human remains. Miners went down – up came a child's skull, a girl's jawbone, and part of a woman's leg. There were reports of a skeleton, with more bones from a baby and young child.

Chief Constable Wilkie ordered remains to be left in the shaft, until police officers were able to go down and make a complete examination. Bad weather hampered the search. On 28 May the recovery attempts failed, due to an inrush of water caused by heavy rain on Saturday. More powerful pumping machinery was ordered. The police were keen to find any remaining hair. Hair preserves well, and could be a crucial element in identification. A retired Oldham mining engineer volunteered his services, and more powerful pumping equipment came from nearby collieries. The remains were found and recovered. One policeman, Sam Roe, was at the scene throughout the recovery. He had come close to death when the lifting tackle holding him up from the pit bottom almost broke, pitching him down towards the water. Fortunately for him, the rope did not entirely break, so his life was saved.

The Coroner's Inquest opened on 11 June. The remains were alleged to be of Hannah Calladine and her two children, Elsie and Albert Edward Burrows, whose father and namesake, already charged with Tommy's murder, was present in court. The 62-year-old suspect wore a dark blue suit and was described as having a 'quiet demeanour'.

A witness, Eliza Hammond, said she last saw Hannah on 11 January 1920. Next day she saw Burrows, who said, 'I have been taking Elsie to her mother.' Eliza asked where they had gone. 'It is a secret between me and her never to tell. The children will be all right, as I have found them a good home, and they will never trouble me any more for anything.'

Eliza later received a postcard signed 'Nance', allegedly from Hannah. She told Burrows that she believed he had sent it.

To ensure a foolproof case, the police had two medical witnesses, an anatomist and a pathologist. Professor Stopford declared his opinion that the bones were of an adult female and that the number of immature bones were probably those of a child between 3 and 6, and the others of a child in its second year. He could not say how long the bones had been in the pit, but they had been immersed for a long time. He pointed out some identifying marks on Hannah's skull, at which point another witness, Hannah's sister, Margaret, became rather ill and had to leave the courtroom.

His colleague, Dr Dible, a pathologist, stated that there was an almost complete female skeleton, a nearly complete skeleton of a 4-year-old child, and some bones from a younger child. Hannah's sister had recovered, and was able to identify some of the clothes. She had made them for Elsie, her niece. Hannah's boots had also been recovered. They were identified as hers, made for her by a Nantwich boot maker, and purchased from him in Nantwich. Also produced was a letter from Burrows, who was in Strangeways Prison. He had sent it to Mrs Calladine, Hannah's mother. In it he asked Mrs Calladine to send him details of Hannah's address. He wrote that the family had all been together on 4 March, and 'if Nance [Hannah] had been woman enough to come forward, I would not have been here.'

The inquest was adjourned until the next day. When it reopened more witnesses appeared to confirm the details already set out. Margaret Anne Street, of Glossop, said that, at about 6.30 a.m., she has seen Burrows going down a lane leading to the Simmondley shaft, holding by the hand a little girl of about 4 years old. A few hours later, at 9.30 a.m., she saw Burrows walking back alone. A few days later she saw Burrows in town, who told her, 'Nan has got a good shop with a relative of mine. We've got the children in a good home.'

'So, what are they going to live on?'

'That's between me and Nance,' he replied, 'but they'll never trouble me any more, as they've made up their minds never to come here and bother me again.'

Robert Mellor said that he and his brother were at Glossop railway station, they saw Burrows being led away by the police, and he was heard to shout, 'When I have done my time I will get this woman. I will either do her in or put her down a pit shaft.'

At this point Burrows jumped up and said, 'I want a private conversation with the Chief Constable and Inspector Chadwick.'

'It's all true,' said Mellor.

Burrows replied, 'The inspector knows different. When we got on the platform there was no time for anything. It was a rush to catch the train.'

The coroner said that Burrows had made a remarkable request, but he could say whatever he wanted and was not obliged to say anything against himself. Burrows declared that Mellor had told a pack of lies, and was not even at the station. At the end of the inquest, Burrows was remanded in custody for another week. The coroner's jury had returned a verdict of 'Wilful Murder' on the victims.

Following the Coroner's Court proceedings and verdict, the next step was the Magistrates' Court, held at Glossop Police Court. The hearing opened Tuesday, 19 June 1923, in front of the Mayor. As before, there was a large and hostile crowd outside the court.

A Mr G.R. Paling, who appeared for the Director of Public Prosecutions, said that Hannah Calladine and her two children arrived in Glossop in December 1919 and lived with Burrows at his house, 94b Back Kershaw Street. The woman and her children disappeared in January 1920. In April 1923 the prisoner was charged with the murder of a little boy, Tommy Wood. During his time in prison on remand, a chance remark was made. This prompted the police to re-open the search of the colliery airshaft, and the remains of Hannah and her children were found.

Burrows had met the then Miss Calladine during the war, and although a married man, had made her his mistress and fathered a child with her. The little boy was named after his father, and took his surname. After Miss Calladine had obtained an affiliation order against him (i.e. had sued him for child maintenance) he took her back with him to Glossop. Burrows legally-wed wife then became angry and left him, suing him for maintenance. To add to his problems, Burrows was out of work and greatly in arrears with his rent. The maintenance hearing was to be held on Monday, 12 January 1920. On the evening of the Sunday 11 January, Burrows went for a walk on Glossop Moors with Hannah and little Albert. Neither mother nor child was ever seen again. The prosecution case was that the prisoner had murdered them both and thrown the bodies down a pit shaft on 11 January 1920. The next day, Monday, 12 January 1920, Burrows was seen walking with the little girl, Elsie. He walked back alone. A neighbour, Mrs Hammond, remarked, 'Having your walk early this morning?' Burrows had grunted, 'Yes, I have been taking Elsie to join her mother.'

Mr George Dale, a Glossop newsagent, told how, in the week before the hearing, Burrows had asked him to intercede with his estranged wife, asking her to drop the case.

'You might tell her that Nance has gone. She has gone housekeeping for a widower.'

'What about the kiddies?'

Burrows replied that the new employer had no children and was pleased with them. Burrows also added that if his wife would drop the summons, 'all bother' might be settled and she could come home straight away.

On the day of the maintenance hearing, at about 8.30 a.m., Burrows again saw Mr Dale. He stopped him and asked him to take a note to Mrs Burrows asking her to withdraw the summons and come home. 'No – she's decided to take the case forward.' Burrows was very upset with that news.

Simmondley, near Glossop.

Two Glossop householders said that in January 1920 Burrows called to sell them some children's clothing and boots.

Harold Garside, an employee of a Glossop jeweller, gave evidence that Burrows offered for sale a gold wedding ring in February 1920. The jewellers purchased it for 30s and later resold it for melting down.

The maintenance hearing was heard. Within a week of it, his wife had returned to him. Burrows kept on telling his friends and neighbours that Nance and the children had gone away, and did not want to be contacted. But he told Hannah's relations that she was still living with him. In fact, he even sent a photograph of his nephew in November 1921, explaining that it was Hannah's new-born son.

Upon his arrest for the murder of Tommy Wood, Burrows apparently intended to use the defence that he had taken Tommy onto the moors, where he met Hannah Calladine and his own son, little Albert, who would then have been 4 years old. The two had played together, then he suddenly noticed that Tommy was missing. Burrows realised that, to make the alibi credible, he had to produce the late Hannah Calladine, or give a credible explanation for her non-appearance. When in the prison hospital, on remand, he had asked a fellow prisoner to write a letter in Hannah's name, stating that she was tired of life and 'wanted to do herself in'.

A young woman, Martha Williams, in the custody of two wardresses, gave evidence as to the prisoner and Hannah Calladine having lived as husband and wife at her mother's house in Nantwich. Hannah had been a friend. Just before last Christmas (1922) she had received a letter, purportedly from Hannah, saying:

> I have the best husband and everything I want. All I can say is that I have been a fool taking notice of my sister and parents and in hope I shall never see them again without they speak the truth about my husband. They are not fit to black his boots. I hope to see you soon, your old workmate, Nance at Gadbrook.

A fellow prisoner in Strangeways, John Thomas Rogers, a collier of Ancoats, Manchester, said that while in the prison hospital last March, Burrows had the next bed to him. They got to talking.

'What are you in for?'

'I've been blamed for the murder of a little boy.'

'Did you do it?'

'No,' said Burrows, adding that there was a woman who could get him off the charge if only she would come forward. He went on to say that whilst out with little Tommy, he had met this woman, who also had a little boy with her. The two boys went off playing together and after some time the other little boy came back, saying that Tommy had fallen through a hole in the wall at the top of the pit shaft. The woman went to look down the shaft. Burrows said he told the woman to go, as he did not want his wife to know that he had been with her, nor did he want his daughter to know that he had been married bigamously to that woman (Hannah). Burrows said that he left the woman, and went to Tommy Wood's mother. He told her that her little boy was lost, and joined the search party.

By May 1923, as Rogers' sentence was coming to an end, Burrows asked him a favour.

'Could you write a letter to me and post it from Crewe?'

'What do you want me to write,' asked Rogers. Burrows wrote on slate an example of Hannah's handwriting.

'Write it like this, and say, "I and the children are all right. Hoping to see you soon" and sign it "Hannah Calladine" and put some crosses on the bottom.'

Rogers said that Burrows promised him some money for writing the letter, if he got off. Rogers said yes, but admitted he had no intention of writing any such letter.

The Assize trial opened at Glossop on Tuesday, 3 July 1923, before Mr Justice Shearman. After all the evidence from the Coroner's Inquest and preliminary hearings, it was something of an anti-climax. However, there were sixty witnesses for the prosecution. The prosecution counsel was Sir Henry Maddocks, KC MP, whilst Burrows had the services of Mr T.N. Winning, and his assistant Miss Geike-Cobb.

After the prosecution had outlined its case, Mr Winning tried his best to put forward his client's defence case.

Mr Winning pointed out one fact in his client's favour: Hannah's sister had identified a blue skirt found in the pit shaft as one she had sent to Hannah in a trunk. That trunk was proven to have arrived on 15 January, four days after the supposed murder. It was hard to suppose that Burrows would have gone over the moors in mid-winter to drop a dress down a pit shaft. Mr Winning also pointed out that Hannah was the mother of two illegitimate children, had a bigamous marriage, and was affected with other unfortunate circumstances, so she had probably committed suicide.

Mr Winning was on a losing streak. After a short absence, the jury returned a verdict of 'Guilty'.

On being asked if he had anything to say, Burrows said, 'I am not afraid of death, but I am not guilty. I loved those children, and the woman too. As I hope to meet my God I am innocent.' The death sentence was then passed upon him. The judge then agreed with the prosecution counsel that public thanks be given to PC Sam Roe for his valiant efforts at the pit shaft.

Burrows was never tried for the murder of Tommy Wood, and never gave an explanation for that crime, so the details and motives for his murder remain unknown.

Attempts were made to get a reprieve for Burrows on the grounds that he was mentally unstable at the time of the murder. The appeals fell on deaf ears and the Home Secretary allowed the execution to take place. Burrows was executed at Bagthorpe Gaol, Nottingham on Wednesday, 8 August 1923. The hangman was John Ellis, the assistant William Willis.

BIBLIOGRAPHY

Many works were consulted in making this book. This is only a short list of some of the most useful sources.

BOOKS
Goodman, Jonathan, *The Stabbing of George Henry Storrs* Allison & Busby, 1983
Hayhurst, Alan, *Cheshire Murders*, Sutton Publishing, 2006
James, R.W., *To the Best of Your Skill and Knowledge: A Short History of the Cheshire Police 1857-1957*
Vincent, B., *Haydn's Dictionary of Dates and Universal Information*, 25th ed., Ward, Lock & Co., London, 1910
Yarwood, Derek, *Cheshire's Execution Files*, Breedon Books Publishing, 2007

NEWSPAPERS
Crewe Guardian
Chester Chronicle
London Gazette
The Times (London)
The Manchester Guardian
Stockport Advertiser

OFFICIAL DOCUMENTS
The Annual Register

Other titles published by The History Press

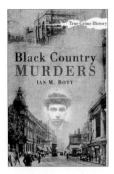

Black Country Murders

IAN M. BOTT

Contained within these pages are the stories behind some of the most heinous crimes ever committed in the Black Country. Ian M. Bott re-examines the cases, some almost forgotten by the ravages of time, and most untold or unpublished since they were first sensationalised in newspapers contemporary to their time. All manner of murder and mystery is featured here, and this book is sure to be a must-read for true crime enthusiasts everywhere.

978 0 7509 5053 4

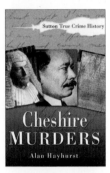

Cheshire Murders

ALAN HAYHURST

Some of the gruesome cases in this book are better known than others, such as the inexplicable shooting by Lock Ah Tam of his wife and two daughters in 1926 and the Gorse Hall murder in 1909. Others are less well known, including the mysterious murder of Mary Malpas in 1835 and the tale of the 'Congleton Cannibal'.

978 0 7509 4076 4

Hanged at Manchester

STEVE FIELDING

The history of execution at Manchester began with the hanging of a young Salford man, convicted of murdering a barman on Boxing Day 1868. Over the next ninety-five years many infamous criminals took the short walk to the gallows. They included Dr Buck Ruxton, who butchered his wife and maid; John Jackson, who escaped from Strangeways after murdering a prison warder; and Walter Rowland, hanged for the murder of a prostitute. Steve Fielding has fully researched all these cases, and they are collected together here in one volume for the first time.

978 0 7509 5052 7

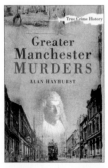

Greater Manchester Murders

ALAN HAYHURST

Contained within the pages of this book are the stories behind some of the most notorious murders in the history of Greater Manchester. They include the case of notorious cat burglar Charlie Peace, who killed 20-year-old PC Nicholas Cook in Seymour Grove, and only confessed when he had already been sentenced to death for another murder; and the sad tale of William Robert Taylor, whose young daughter was killed in a boiler explosion and whom, later, desperate and in debt, murdered a bailiff as well as his three remaining children.

978 0 7509 5091 6

Visit our website and discover thousands of other History Press books.

www.thehistorypress.co.uk